Coming to Age

Marie-Louise von Franz, Honorary Patron

**Studies in Jungian Psychology
by Jungian Analysts**

Daryl Sharp, General Editor

COMING TO AGE

The Croning Years
and
Late-Life Transformation

Jane R. Prétat

To Alma Paulsen-Hoyer who, at a critical juncture between
my midlife and croning years, helped me find the analyst
in myself and showed me that the hard work of individuation
is lifelong, as is the pleasure and creativity.

Canadian Cataloguing in Publication Data

Prétat, Jane R., 1926-
    Coming to age: the croning years and late-life transformation

(Studies in Jungian psychology by Jungian analysts; 62)

Includes bibliographical references and index.

ISBN 978-0-919123-63-2

1. Aging—Psychological aspects.
2. Middle age—Psychological aspects.
3. Aged—Psychology.
4. Jung, C.G. (Carl Gustav), 1875-1961.
I. Title.   II. Series.

BF724.55.A35P74 1994   155.67   C93-094819-X

INNER CITY BOOKS
Box 1271, Station Q, Toronto, ON M4T 2P4, Canada
Telephone (416) 927-0355
FAX (416) 924-1814

Honorary Patron: Marie-Louise von Franz.
Publisher and General Editor: Daryl Sharp.
Senior Editor: Victoria Cowan.

INNER CITY BOOKS was founded in 1980 to promote the
understanding and practical application of the work of C.G. Jung.

Cover: "Reflections on Alex," oil on linen, 40" x 34".
Copyright © 1989 by Nancy C. Witt.

Printed and bound in Canada by
Thistle Printing Limited

CONTENTS

See final page for descriptions of other Inner City Books

Acknowledgments

I would like to thank David Tresan, who delivered a paper at the 1990 Ghost Ranch Conference in which he mentioned the possibility of a late-life *metanoia* as it manifested in Jung's sixties. This produced an "aha!" in me and gave me the focus I needed for my own ideas.

I would also like to thank those who have fed both my body and my mind unstintingly at important times. Linda Carter, Joe Cambray, Jackie Schectman and Margaret Smalzel are only four of many. They have been there when I needed relationship and tactfully understood when I didn't. Many of the basic concepts in this book have been informed over the years through dialogue with other analysts and teachers at the C.G. Jung Institute in Boston. Their input has been invaluable.

David Hart deserves special mention for his quiet understanding and his gentle, unobtrusive nurturance of the seed of this book.

Many extraordinary elders of generations now gone, my parents and grandparents among them, have contributed more than I can say to my understanding of the crone in her incredible variety of forms. A special place goes to Hansi Greer who was my first Jungian teacher until her death just before her eightieth birthday.

Several anonymous persons who have allowed their stories and dreams to be added to these pages deserve a very special mention. Their permission to share the richness of their experience is a gift to us all.

My editors have been both a joy and a challenge. I feel enormously grateful to Daryl Sharp and Victoria Cowan of Inner City Books, and to Suzi Naiburg in Cambridge. They have patiently borne with me through the ascents and descents of getting a manuscript ready to be published.

My three-generation family has challenged and sustained me through many years of Jungian work. I feel proudly grateful that we have survived the trials of family relationships and are still part of each other's lives.

Last but not least I wish to thank those who have pondered and constructively criticized this work as it progressed. Their names would fill pages. Special thanks to Dian Reynolds who did some of the original editing, to Susannne Short who first encouraged me to turn the original into a book, and to Robert Bosnak, who fathered it into the world with his ongoing support.

Introduction

Our lives are always changing. Daily, even hourly, the cells of our bodies transform. No matter how hard we try to keep things the same, programming ourselves to maintain the status quo, alterations in our psyches are always underway. Sometimes these changes are so subtle and gradual that we hardly notice. Other times they explode into our lives in ways we can't ignore. The tiny, subtle changes we take for granted, yet they too can throw us off balance in painful and disorienting ways. New integration is necessarily preceded by disintegration. If things are to come together in a new way, they must first come apart.

One major change is just beginning to arouse attention. In the years between middle and old age, the time of life when we are no longer in our prime but not yet truly old, most of us undergo a transition. Both body and soul stand on the threshold of age. Between our fifties and our seventies we are called to undergo a most profound transformation. Life changes radically, and so do we—physically, psychologically, mentally and spiritually. That, it seems, is both our hope and our fear.

C.G. Jung used the word *metanoia* to describe the deep change of attitude that can result from a period of trauma and psychological upheaval.[1] While he wrote about *metanoia* as the outcome of his own midlife crises, it seems today to be equally if not more applicable to what I term "the croning years," the years of coming to age. Modern health care has made it possible to prolong not only our lives, but also our vitality. Hence we who are now in our fifties and sixties may well be the first generation in history that is neither young nor old for about twenty or twenty-five years of our post-midlives.

My purpose in this book is not to develop a methodology for

---

[1] *Symbols of Transformation,* CW 5, p. xxvi. [CW refers throughout to *The Collected Works of C.G. Jung*]

dealing with the rewards and challenges of the later years. Instead I will look at those attitudes that can guide us to creatively affirm our destiny and, in Jung's words, to "forge an ego . . . that endures the truth."[2]

In the Western world aging is not generally considered a cause for celebration. While honored in some societies, all too often we North Americans view it as abhorrent. Getting older, we joke, is just a bit better than the alternative. One wonders if someday aging might even show up on the diagnostic list of characterological disorders! Everywhere we turn we hear that it's healthier to stay young. Billions of dollars are spent annually on the quest for youthful appearance, ability and attitude.

When people who have lived by such values first discover themselves neither young nor old, neither middle aged nor yet elders, they may feel depressed, sure that they have lost their identity. The old persona masks no longer fit. The youthful face and figure, the former acuity of mind, the stamina and flexibility of the body, all seem to be vanishing. Sexual seductiveness, even if present, is no longer the same. In fact aging individuals may feel so different that they start secretly wandering in strange inner landscapes, searching in vain for understanding of their feelings of disorientation.

For those acculturated to value the beauty, sexuality and style of young adulthood, this is a difficult time. Like the Greek goddess Demeter whose maiden aspect was abducted into the underworld, aging humans begin to mourn their lost youth. As if seared by their grief, the world seems to dry up around them. We may act as we did before, but as we realize our aging we're apt to stand with the crone-goddess Demeter/Hecate at a crossroads, mourning. Every road suddenly seems to lead only toward increasing deprivation. Each way holds only a bewildering loss of youthful dreams. As one woman lamented, "I've lost it and it's not coming back."

When we realize that we no longer measure our lives in years since birth but now carefully estimate the unknowable number of

---

[2] *Memories, Dreams, Reflections,* p. 297.

years left before death, our zest for life may vanish, desire and determination evaporate. The years to come may well be numerous, but in despair the end feels imminent. With no understanding, no way of knowing that the death we shiver against in the wee hours could be symbolic or even the first stage of a new beginning, sleep eludes us and waking dread take its place. No one tells us that it might be our old way of being in the world that must die to make way for the new. Left with only the feeling that creativity and juiciness are mysteriously lost, we feel bereft.

As we stand on the threshold of the last phase of our lives, nothing seems to work anymore, no matter how hard we try. Both the approach of old age and the deterioration of our bodies seem loathsome. In fright, we run off into frantic activity, becoming too busy to think, or sink deeper and deeper into a paralyzing depression. Only rarely do we have the wisdom to honor our changes and allow their development. Most of us, unguided and untaught, flee in fear from the life that precedes our old age and death.

I have been surprised by the dearth of material about the approach to age as a developmental task. While the subject of midlife crisis has been thoroughly analyzed, little has been said about descents and returns in the years after. Gerontologists have studied old age extensively, but few have given attention to the "betwixt and between" years of people in their fifties and sixties. People in this age group are neither middle aged nor elderly. They are a population unto themselves. Yet little is addressed specifically to or about them.

Today in the Western world the human life span is increasing, and as it does, the need grows for a deeper wisdom that can help older persons honor rather than deny the physical and psychological relinquishings that precede a late blooming. The threshing and tempering of such a time can be overwhelming. Not only is our conscious and habitual perception of ourselves, built up over the course of our lives, being sorely tried, but psyche and soma are also being tested in ways that can be extremely painful. We're not sure we like it, but we are in transition whether we like it or not. Our lives are changing. Yet no one tells us how to relate to these changes. We look for answers but find little information. As Jane Wheelwright, an analyst in her eighties, tells us, older persons may well wonder, "Where are the guidelines for us as individuals? They will find that there are none."[3]

Where then can we look for knowledge? How do we find affirmation for the difficult work of our croning years?

Jungian analysts seem uniquely able to speak to the questions posed by life passages. We emphasize the importance of honoring symptoms, especially conflict and depression, while attending psyche, waiting for an individual solution to emerge. Frequently out of the mainstream in supporting introversion and descent into the unconscious as important tasks, Jungian analysts see stress and symptom as necessary elements of initiation into new ways of being. This perspective is especially suited to older persons who over the years have developed a strong ego and lived out some of the goals of earlier life stages.

In the first chapter I shall describe and define what is meant by the profound change, or *metanoia,* to which the trials of the croning years can lead. Chapter two considers what happened to Jung in his late fifties and sixties. The experiences of Jung and the two most significant women in his life can give us important insight into what it means to stay with the chaos of late-life change until a new attitude is born from the depths of psyche.

In chapter three I look at the transition of the croning years and what it means to many men and women who are coming to age. As we shall see in chapter four, psychologists, anthropologists and gerontologists have explored old age, and some of their ideas also apply to the transitional years just before.

Much of the personal work in the croning years is with the body. Chapter five specifically deals with the aging body—both physical and imaginal. The body of the person coming to age contains memories, perhaps trauma, and an immune system that is diminished as well as physical symptoms which echo psychological disease. The aging body can also be the source of creativity and new life energy

---

[3] *For Women Growing Older,* p. 44.

waiting to be released. One way of aiding this release is through a technique that Jung called active imagination. Chapter six provides examples of active imagination with the body, suggesting some new ways to relate to our physical selves as we age and change.

In chapter seven the crone shows herself in both her positive and negative aspects, opening up our ideas about aging. Over centuries of denigration of the feminine the word "crone" lost any positive value. The good qualities of the old woman disappeared into what Marie-Louise von Franz calls "the white shadow,"[4] repressed and hidden, so that only the dark side has been available to consciousness. What would it be like to redeem that shadow and acknowledge the postive qualities of the crone?

Chapter eight tells the story of Demeter and her search for her lost youth and creativity. Her myth tells of a periodic return of what has disappeared into the underworld. Demeter's daughter is carried off a maiden and returns a queen. Similarly our own creative energy may descend into the unconscious leaving us bereft. Yet this same energy can return renewed, enriched by its time in darkness.

In our croning years we are explorers of a stage of life that is different than it was for previous generations. The years of coming to age are now a new challenge and like most challenges bring the stresses of relinquishing familiar ways. Going through the changes of this time can be as exciting and as difficult as any outer journey. Those of us now coming to age are pathfinders, hopefully marking a way for others to follow.

---

[4] *Shadow and Evil in Fairy Tales,* p. 64.

1

Changes

Times of transition are times of testing. This seems particularly true in the croning years when alterations in our bodies, our psyches and our circumstances repeatedly challenge us. The world around us is altered as old settings vanish to make way for new, old friends depart or become strangers, and familiar roles fall away to leave us naked and exposed. New patterns, new mores and new tasks make it difficult to recognize ourselves.

When these events occur, we may try to cope in one of several ways. We may retreat in fear from upheaval in our lives, feeling disoriented and out of control. We may armor ourselves for battle and try to destroy our suffering. We may deny that anything is happening to us. Or we may sink into depression and be unable to do much more than get out of bed. Healthy accommodation and transformation are also possibilities, of course. If coping is difficult, however, we are likely to lose our awareness that such difficulty can bring meaning to our lives. As Ann, an analysand in her mid-sixties, complained, "I open the draperies in the morning and close them at night and in between there is only an aching sense of how much I've lost and how stupid and empty my life has become."

Her children were grown and gone. Her closest friend had died. Others had moved away to new jobs or warmer climates. Because of an old injury, Ann was no longer able to be athletically active. Rocky for years, her marriage had settled into an accommodating friendship with little more than a house and occasional meals shared. Visits from her grandchildren once or twice a year brought some love into Ann's life, but could not keep her day-to-day existence from becoming so humdrum that she marked time only by the ritual act of opening and closing her windows. Ann was unaware that there was meaning in this act, that it had symbolic significance, until in analysis she began to experience the struggle to open and close herself. Only then did her instinctive act begin to make sense.

When we are lost in empty lives, it's hard to hear the instinctual voice, sometimes so deeply implanted that we're barely aware of it, that tells us almost in a whisper the great secret—that the trials of our most disorienting experiences are slowly working on us to transform our consciousness. It's as if we were caught in a darkened vestibule between an old way of being and a new. The doors of the past close behind us. The doors to the future are still unopened. Too often we forget that only by enduring our time in the liminal space between those doors, waiting for an opening, can we eventually move freely across a threshold into the future. When we are stuck and lost in between, we need someone to tell us that within the vestibule we'll find a unique opportunity to learn who we may become. If we can endure with patience and courage until the moment when our lives open to new possibilities, we may regain our energy and chance to grow.

Jung paid special attention to such times of change in his own life and in the lives of his analysands. He wrote about the transformation of consciousness that followed midlife crises, including his own major change of attitude during his sixties and early seventies, following the trauma of illness and war. He saw it as a time of initiation which established a new relationship between his personal ego and the Self.[5] He called this profound transformation *metanoia*.[6] This Greek word has two roots; *meta* meaning both "great change" and "beyond," and *noia*, a derivative of *nous*, a word of complex and multiple meanings, including "higher consciousness."[7]

In a Gnostic creation myth that echoes the Narcissus story, *Nous* is a spark of the Divine that breaks free in the Upper Regions. Looking down from the Heavens, he sees his own reflection mirrored back to him from far below in the dark chaos of *Physis*, the essence of matter. *Physis*, in her turn and out of her own longing and empti-

---

[5] *Memories, Dreams, Reflections*, pp. 289ff.

[6] *Symbols of Transformation*, CW 5, p. xxvi.

[7] See W.S. Hanbrich, *Medical Meanings: A Glossary of Word Origins*, p. 151.

ness, opens herself and welcomes this spark into her depths. Joining, they bring about the first Creation.[8]

The coupling of *Physis* and *Nous* is symbolic of sexual union as well as of a divine marriage of opposites in the psyche. *Metanoia* may be seen therefore as a great coming together of what has previously been polarized, a union of opposites within ourselves beyond anything we have previously experienced. This union creates a new awareness that slowly grows to consciousness within our embodied selves. A spark of something numinous impregnates the vast unformed darkness of the unconscious, gestating new understanding, slowly taking form within chaos. During a time of liminality and confusion, we await this birth, sometimes with joy but also with dread of the unknown.

There are times when the birth of new consciousness comes suddenly in a life-changing epiphany. More often it happens slowly, preceded by a long period in which the darkness seems hopelessly black and growth of the seed of creative energy almost imperceptible. We are pregnant with new content that we can neither see nor comprehend. To quote one version of the Book of John: "And the light shone in the darkness, and the darkness could not comprehend it."[9]

Any transition can present us with the opportunity for a major change. As Jung has told us, midlife is one such time. Coming to age is another. Less familiar but perhaps even more demanding, the years in which we are neither middle aged nor yet old present us with repeated challenges to change at the very time when we feel we are getting too old or too set in our ways to do so.

The threshold time before old age is unknown territory for most of us. In the past decade a great deal of work has been focused on the middle years. The C.G. Jung Foundation in New York, for example, recently inaugurated a program of midlife studies. Recent books on this subject include Murray Stein's *In Midlife*, James Hollis's *The Middle Passage* and Daryl Sharp's *The Survival Papers*. Far less has

---

[8] See *Aion,* CW 9ii, par. 368.
[9] John 1:5 (Self Pronouncing Edition, National Bible Press, ca. 1930).

been written about the period of life that leads up to old age. As Stein points out, the subject of age is still psychologically virgin territory.[10] In much of contemporary literature, the time of coming to age gets lumped in with midlife issues as if one truly went directly from midlife into old age. Many of us in our late fifties and sixties disagree, asserting that we are neither middle aged nor elderly but rather live in an undefined area between the two, where some days we feel all the energy of youth and others all the deficits of age.[11]

Midlife *metanoia* is a cause for rejoicing. It is similar to a time described in the Bible when the desert blooms and the voice of the turtle dove is heard in the land. It's easy to feel that our work is done, our goals reached, and our personality transformed once and for all when we've successfully navigated the crisis of midlife. Libido flows into life like fresh water rising up from a deep well.

At forty-five Dorie emerged from a long midlife descent with new energy and drive. "Tell me it will never be that bad again," she pleaded as we ended our work together. She felt that she had come to know many of the strengths and weaknesses of her shadow. She was more assertive and had more self-confidence. To quote Polly Young-Eisendrath and Florence Wiedemann, she had "confronted darkness and strengthened her courage by honestly facing shameful and aggressive self-images," and had "lived through the fatigue, depression, and anxiety generated by both necessary work in the world and her own self-reflective process of development."[12]

Balancing family, career and her own inner process had often seemed overwhelming and impossible for Dorie, but she had survived and grown through her struggles. Now she had a new job that energized and nourished her. Her interaction with her teen-aged children had improved as she was able to give them more autonomy. Her relationship with her husband, while not easy, was more honest and supportive of them both. Dorie felt a sense of accomplishment

---

[10] *In Midlife*, p. 3.

[11] See Rosemary Gordon, *Dying and Creating: A Search for Meaning.*

[12] *Female Authority: Empowering Women Through Psychotherapy,* p. 214.

and excitement about the future. We ended our work together with a feeling of satisfaction and completion.

I was tempted to reassure her by saying that surely she would never have another descent quite as bad. She had, after all, triumphed in her journey into the unconscious. She was a survivor. Yet I feel quite sure that in all probability Dorie will experience another period of trial, perhaps even more profound. As releasing and healing as a midlife *metanoia* can be, it nevertheless can be what the alchemists termed "a first whitening," an albedo, a preliminary stage in the individuation process.[13] It's likely that sometime between her mid-fifties and early seventies, Dorie's life energy will once again descend into the unconscious so that she will experience depression or ennui as another initiation and another *metanoia* is precipitated.

Interviews with elders confirm that many experience a descent leading to a major change. Biographies of famous people often show a late blooming that follows crisis in the sixth or seventh decade. It is quite clear from Jung's letters that he emerged from this transition to do some of his most important work in alchemy. *Mysterium Coniunctionis* and *Aion,* works of his later life, are a rich legacy for those who work with archetypal material.

Jung developed his own rituals for his aging years. In his sixties he spent time close to the earth and to Lake Zürich, in Küsnacht and in his tower at Bollingen. He sailed his boat and worked in his garden. He added to Bollingen, remarking that as psyche expanded so did his tower. He carved stone and read alchemy. He realized too that his illnesses were initiations into age and a new attitude toward life and death. Without much outward ceremony, and quite privately, he managed to create ritual acts to mark his turning points.

Some societies still enact initiatory ceremonies such as rites for pubescent boys, who are taken from the mothers' area by the men of certain tribes and put through trials that mark them, often physically, as grown males. Victor Turner in his studies of primitive initiations

---

[13] See "The Psychology of the Transference," *The Practice of Psychotherapy,* CW 16, par. 484.

called the time between adolescence and young adulthood "betwixt and between" or "liminal" time.[14] *Limin* is Latin for threshold. Life transitions, Turner writes, are times of standing on the threshold of change. Both Turner and Murray Stein note that the initiate standing in liminal space may feel foggy and disoriented.[15] I use the term "late-liminal" for the trials of later life, because it describes so aptly that threshold between the old way of being and the new.

Our society has few rites of passage for the threshold times of age. While we've retained some of our rites of adolescence and youth, such as Bar/Bat Mitzvah and marriage ceremonies, we seem somewhat embarrassed about late-life rituals. Many of us would have to confess that while we long for ceremony to mark our passage into age, we would feel rather self-conscious about participating in the men's or women's groups that are trying to recover some of the old modes of celebration like "cronings" or accessing the wild woman or wild man within. While we may admire the free access to humor of a mythic figure like Baubo, the woman who made Demeter laugh with her raunchy humor, the urge to Victorian propriety is still strong in most of us. We can't really let go in public or celebrate an aging process we've learned to abhor. Yet we know instinctually that change is in our bodies, in our daily activities and in our dreams.

We live in a culture bare of transforming rituals. Yet psychological development seems to require them. As London analyst Anthony Stevens writes:

> Archetypal symbols of initiation arise spontaneously in dreams at critical periods in the life-cycle—at puberty, betrothal, marriage, childbirth, at divorce, separation, or death of a spouse, at the betrothal and marriage of one's children, at the approach of old age and death. . . . It seems that the attainment of a new stage of life demands that the initiation symbols appropriate to that stage must be experienced. If culture fails to provide these symbols in institutional form then the Self is forced to provide them *faute de mieux.*[16]

---

[14] See "Betwixt and Between: The Liminal Period in *Rites de Passage.*"
[15] *In Midlife: A Jungian Perspective,* p. 9.
[16] *Archetypes: A Natural History of the Self,* p. 164.

As we move toward a late-life *metanoia,* it seems that we must develop rituals to alleviate the confusion and despair we experience on leaving the safety of habitual ways. Consciously or unconsciously we do enact ritual moments that often are provided by the Self, archetype of wholeness and regulating center of the psyche. Like Ann, we mark the passage of light and dark in our homes. As we move from past to future, we may start wearing new colors, stop dying our hair, start keeping a dream journal, take a trip, study nature, investigate old religions and myths, plant new gardens, develop new relationships. Frequently our bodies get into the act and say "pay attention to me" by developing symptoms we can't ignore. These aches and pains, too, may have a symbolic or ritual quality.

Rituals seem to be especially important to the feminine in men as well as in women. Perhaps this has something to do with the need to enact our relationship to the community. While great strides have been made in the quest for equality, women, and especially older women, are still often treated as second-class citizens. Men and women alike, we are all too often the victims of an outdated patriarchy. Women are victims of men—collectively and individually—but also of our own saturnine masculinity that doggedly hangs on to outdated standards of behavior and appearance. The late-liminal time is especially trying for those who have been traditionally acculturated to identify with their persona, the way they appear to others. Many older men are attempting to find their own way past the masks they've always worn, to connect with emotions they have traditionally projected onto mothers, sisters or wives. Many older women are still struggling to establish their own identity, to have their own thoughts, having traditionally seen themselves primarily as someone's daughter, wife or mother.

With or without ritual, women who have passed midlife and initial menopause cannot deny the changes in their bodies and their psyches, as well as in the ways they are perceived in the world. What the changes mean is all too often unclear.

Until recently few older women came to therapy and even fewer aging men. Perhaps this is one reason why so little has been written about a late-life *metanoia*. For many who grew up before or during the Second World War, therapy is an unlikely choice. While some made the transition smoothly and didn't need help, many suffered. The "pull yourself-up-by-the-bootstraps" philosophy passed down by Victorian parents often left them awash in a sea of depression. Even today it can be astonishing to discover the suffering behind the careful masks of men and women taught lifelong to smile, to endure through pain. The courage with which they get out of bed and face each new day is remarkable. Dyed hair or careful makeup, the self-abnegation and self-inflicted sarcasms of some and the curt bossiness and rigidity of others are all learned behaviors, coping skills society has taught them to use to keep ego and their old self-image alive.

We've all seen the ill effects of alcohol used as a buoy to keep some elders afloat. We've also seen others flounder, wondering why they felt ill and off balance, making the rounds of physicians to try to find some physical cause for their distress. Until the latter part of this century, it was the exceptional medical doctor who could see symbolic meaning or purpose in the array of symptoms their older patients presented, or understand that "somatizing," "nerves" or "hypochondria" might have deeper meanings and shouldn't be dismissed summarily as temporary neuroses common to those who are aging.

Today more and more older people are seeking appropriate psychotherapy. In spite of the prejudices of a culture oriented to a quick fix, a painless solution, a psychic antibiotic to cure the virus of depression, older men and women are coming to Jungian analysis in increasing numbers. Many want to work on their dreams and are strong enough and imaginative enough to profit greatly from depth psychology. Many not only have the ability to do the work but also a solidity of personality that has developed over a lifetime.

It is an easy trap to see the disorientation of an aging person in transition as pathological or as a contraindication for depth work. The symptoms for which our patients seek a quick solution may not respond well to a lecture on the importance of optimism or a prescription for a psychotropic drug. Instead, their pain and distress may be calling them to undergo an initiatory journey that could change their lives, ushering them into a more fruitful old age as well as a new acceptance of their inevitable physical death.

Frequently I find myself wondering if a subtle age discrimination on the part of therapists and analysts hasn't sometimes contributed to attitudes that have left many in their fifties and sixties unaware that feelings of imminent death and painful somatic symptoms are not abnormal. There is always the danger of unwittingly adding to a person's resistance by pathologizing the disorientation characteristic of the late-liminal transition. It takes time for one to realize that depression and physical distress may be crucial milestones on a major journey inward. Part of our task as guides is to help them recognize in their symptoms a prescription for a descent into another world, the Land of the Mothers, the unconscious, in search of what Patricia Berry calls "our invisible mother in the underworld"—

> the Persephone who rules over the soul in its essential, limiting and immaterial patterns; and that original mother of all Gaia—she who is Earth and yet, without contradiction, that deeper ground of support beneath the earth's physical appearance the non-being beneath and within being.[17]

Berry's concept speaks to our time and particularly to those who are searching so diligently for their roots, struggling to recapture an affirming sense of the feminine. While modern-day efforts to find the *mater* who is the essence of matter have transformed many lives, it is important to remind ourselves that these are outer concretizations of an inner need to find our own connection to the archetypal Mother, the unconscious.

As we turn our attention to psyche, images begin to emerge out of that deepest unknown. While some of these images may seem terrifying and/or destructive, they also can be initiatory guides to a future *metanoia*. Often the most terrifying dreams contain symbolic messages that are just what the dreamer needs. The most benign dreams may be powerful road signs. Sometimes the scariest or most embarrassing dreams contain age-old images of great meaning. Freud was

---

[17] "What's the Matter With Mother?" in *Fathers and Mothers*, p. 101.

correct in attributing enormous importance to sexual symbols. It is far too easy, however, to interpret these symbols only concretely and to miss the message they present of an archetypal urge to join the opposites within the psyche.

William, just turned sixty, talks repeatedly about his desire to have sex with his wife in their hot tub, wondering why it makes him so "unreasonably" angry that she refuses. Without any knowledge of the alchemical images that depict the joining of male and female in a ritual bath, William is embarrassed and apologetic about both his desire and his anger. Once he understands that his desire for such sex is also a longing to ritually act out an unconscious joining of masculine and feminine elements of his own psyche, he is able to talk to his wife about what the act means to him and she becomes less threatened by what she had previously seen as salacious advances.

Sexual desire does often change with age. Foreplay may need more time and attention. When this is misunderstood, it can be interpreted as the need to replace an old lover with one who is younger. When seen as a natural part of aging, slowing down can enrich a relationship in which life history and friendship are shared. Then the desire to experiment, like William's desire for sex in the hot tub, may arise. Understanding the symbolic meaning of such desires can add the richness of a new experience between partners.

Despite the drawbacks of aging, the late-liminal period can usher in a new sense of freedom and individuality. Many of us are drawn to the kind of deepening of understanding that William experienced, or to the freedom of women who begin to enjoy the sensuousness of their bodies. Older people may improvise more, no longer feeling the need to honor past, and frequently dysfunctional, family patterns. Not threatened by an appearance of incompetence or ineptness, they can give up much of their past need for perfection. They may become bolder in affirming their differentness, feel truer to their own being, worry less about pleasing others. They even dare to be outrageous, to adopt personas that suit their personal tastes rather than collective standards.

One woman reported:

I work with my body now rather than against it. It has taken amazingly good care of me all these years. Even my illnesses seem now to have been a kind of care taking that kept me in myself. Now I feel like it's my turn to return the favor. So I get massage, and I exercise, and I try to eat the foods that nourish my body. I'm not always successful at this, but my body and I have developed pretty good communication and if I mess up, she lets me know in a hurry!

While late-life *metanoia* may usher in a sense of freedom and a respect for embodiment, the liminal time preceding may bring difficulty and pain. We must all experience the losses as well as the gains of these years if we are to age with the fortitude that conscious creativity requires.

In a society where only the young are considered truly alive, and aging is dismissed as death's waiting room, many elders experience extreme difficulty with the restlessness and lack of value they sense in themselves and their surroundings. This is exacerbated by a culture that views death as final rather than transformative, leaving us with a barely bridled terror of the depression that seems like death at the door.

The trials and sorrow of such an initiatory time are described vividly in a poem from the *Tao de Ching*.

Give up your knowledge, then you shall be free from care!
Between yes and Yes what difference is there?
Between Good and Evil—what is the difference?
Must I revere what others avow?
O, Vastness, have I not yet reached your center?
Other people are happy, as if celebrating a great feast,
As if climbing great towers.
I alone am drifting, waiting for a sign,
Like a baby before it can smile,
Weary as a wanderer who has no home.
Others live with abundance
I alone am forsaken.
Truly I have the heart of a fool!
Chaos! O, Chaos!
The people of the world are clear, so clear!
I alone am a dullard

Sad, so sad,
Restless, alas, as the sea
Driven to and fro by the winds of change.
The people all have tasks.
I alone am idle, different, good for nothing,
—for I value the lavishing Mother.[18]

Truly, as we go through the disorientation that precedes a late-life *metanoia,* many of us do feel restless, driven every which way by the winds of change. We cannot identify ourselves, much less our goals. We are adrift in a vast uncharted sea, waiting for a sign. Worldly accomplishment loses its meaning. We feel like dullards in a world where others appear to know what they're doing. They seem to have answers, to know what is right or wrong, what is good or bad. We see them as rich in knowledge and self-esteem while we feel as needy as newborn babes. When the worldly wisdom we've built up over a lifetime suddenly fails us, when the "lavishing mother" of the unconscious draws us into her depths, we are lost.

How, then, do we affirm a descent into the unconscious when we are in the depths of confusion? Can we accept the reality and importance of a late-liminal change? Who can guide our transits?

Many of the early gerontological studies were based on a medical model that saw prevention and alleviation of symptoms as the goal, thus reinforcing the collective attitude that the best way to deal with age was to avoid its deficits. Recent studies like those of the Women's Collective in Boston seem more oriented to growth and change in the late years.[19] A Conference on Conscious Aging held in New York in the spring of 1992 also supported such an orientation, with speakers Marion Woodman, Joan Halifax and Rabbi Zalman Schacter-Shalomi talking about the place of elders in primitive and modern societies.

Although Jungian analysts—M. Esther Harding, Marie-Louise

---

[18] Lao Tze, *Tao de Ching: The Book of the Way and Its Virtue,* No. 20 (modified by the author).

[19] Paula Doress, Diana Siegal et al, *Ourselves Growing Older: Women Aging with Knowledge and Power.*

von Franz, Irene Claremont de Castillejo and Jane Wheelwright, among others—have not written about the croning years as such, their work offers special wisdom about age and the ancient traditions that honor it.

Particular mention should be made of one of the pioneer Jungian writers on aging, Florida Scott-Maxwell. She was an important part of my own introduction to Jungian thought in the early sixties. Studying gerontology, I came across an article in which she spoke of the need for older people to face the truth "with a shimmer of irony perhaps, and proper modesty in the presence of good and evil."

> The haunting thought is always in our heads that perhaps we know nothing of age. It may all lie ahead, and can only be faced day by day to its unseeable end. Each hour nibbles at our solidity, and we relinquish something in every little humiliation . . . .
>
> If to be tempered in the fires of insight is the task of age, perhaps . . . childlike naturalness is its reward. Though we are aching, inadequate wrecks, there are times when, in our hearts, we are incurably, deliciously young. I have no idea whether we should be or we should not be. Who is to say?[20]

As a girl, I knew the childlike naturalness of my grandmothers and great aunts as they grew older. In their sixties they knew how to play and imagine in ways middle-aged parents had no time or patience to enjoy. Later I recognized this quality in older friends and in some of the women I worked with at a center for retired persons. By that time, of course, I also recognized the struggles, pain and grief that were part of their days.

Jung, too, lived freely in his old age. Many writers have remarked on the infectious quality of his laughter and peasant humor. It is difficult to believe that he could still find time for correspondence and the many pilgrims who sought him out in his later years, but somehow he managed to mentor many, even when he was ill.

As we shall see in the next chapter, Jung's seventh decade was an extremely demanding one. The deaths of the two women who had

---

[20] "We Are the Sum of Our Days."

carried much of his anima or feminine qualities—his wife Emma and his soul-mate Toni Wolff—caused him great pain. A catastrophic series of life-threatening illnesses in his late sixties and early seventies were trials few could withstand. Yet in spite of these losses Jung brought some of his most important work to fruition. As he himself reported, those events helped him to build an ego that could endure the truth and was capable of coping with the world and with fate: "Nothing is disturbed—neither inwardly nor outwardly, for one's own continuity has withstood the current of life and time."[21]

---

[21] *Memories, Dreams, Reflections,* p. 297.

2
Jung's Late-Life Transition

In 1932, when he was fifty-seven, Carl Gustav Jung published an essay, "The Development of Personality." In it he wrote:

> Our personality develops in the course of our life from germs that are hard or impossible to discern, and it is only our deeds that reveal who we are. We are like the sun, which nourishes the life of the earth and brings forth every kind of strange, wonderful, and evil thing. . . . At first we do not know what deeds or misdeeds, what destiny, what good and evil we have in us, and only the autumn can show what the spring has engendered.[22]

Jung had entered his own autumn years. His work had brought him considerable fame. People came from all over the world to consult with him. Some stayed to become his colleagues and helpers. Others, trained in his approach to the psyche, went on to practice and teach his depth psychology in other countries. Those who worked with Jung or with his students soon understood what he meant by the price one must pay for individuation:

> Clearly, no one develops his personality because somebody tells him that it would he useful or advisable to do so. Nature has never yet been taken in by well-meaning advice. . . .
> . . . The development of personality is a favour that must he paid for dearly . . . .
> . . . It also means fidelity to the law of one's own being.[23]

> What is it, in the end, that induces a man to go his own way and to rise out of unconscious identity with the mass as out of a swathing mist? Not necessity, for necessity comes to many and they all take refuge in convention.[24]

---

[22] *The Development of Personality,* CW 17, par. 290.
[23] Ibid., pars. 293ff.
[24] Ibid., par. 299.

It is what is commonly called *vocation:* an irrational factor that destines a man to emancipate himself from the herd and from its well-worn paths. True personality is always a vocation and puts its trust in it as in God. . . . vocation acts like a law of God from which there is no escape.[25]

He also wrote:

Everything could be left undisturbed did not the new way demand to be discovered, and did it not visit humanity with all the plagues of Egypt until it finally is discovered.[26]

These words could almost be taken as premonitory, since Jung was plagued repeatedly in the years ahead. During his sixties and early seventies, he had to cope not only with the stress of a heavy practice and worldwide fame but also with the strain of Nazism beginning to encroach on his native Switzerland. The pressures on him in the late 1930s were similar to those he had experienced at midlife, starting with his visions in 1913, but now he was older and his life had changed considerably. The terrifying dreams and visions he had had in the years leading up to the First World War had plunged him into a time of disorientation and despair.

The outcome of Jung's struggles during those years was a great change of conscious attitude that brought transformation and creativity to his life and work, a midlife *metanoia.* Yet despite the psychological balance he had achieved, Jung was again intensely challenged and tested in his sixties, as his letters from 1935 to 1945 show. The stresses he suffered had a different effect this time but certainly were no easier to bear.

In Jung's midlife dreams and visions Europe ran with blood and old war-loving gods rode to battle in the skies. At the time Jung felt jeopardized by warring factions in his own psyche. Only later was he able to see the synchronicity linking his experiences and what was about to happen in the outer world. It seems apparent that in 1913 he hadn't yet come to terms with the mystic in himself. The paintings he

---

[25] Ibid., par. 300.
[26] Ibid., par. 323.

did during this time reveal the almost overwhelming power that unconscious forces had in his life as he underwent midlife change.[27]

During Jung's sixties, pressures of work and war took their toll in a different way. New crises arose, but this time the struggle seems to have been more with his body and its reaction to the upheaval in his outer life. Some of his somatizing may have been a response to the stresses of another war. Some was the struggle to cope with aging and with losses. It is not unusual for a late-liminal crisis to take physical form, forcing us to pay attention to our bodies in new ways while at the same time the changes in our bodies force us to pay new attention to our psyche. It seems to be a necessary task of individuation to come to terms with one's own physical being. Sometimes this takes the form of a serious illness. Joan Halifax's work with elder healers among the rain forest people has convinced her that shamen usually undergo severe physical trials in their training as part of a deconstruction phase preceding new integration.[28]

In the years between his thirties and his sixties Jung had worked productively, writing, analyzing patients, building the first sections of the tower at Bollingen that he realized mirrored his own psychic growth. His five children had grown and he had seven grandchildren. He had become president of the International Society for Psychotherapy, traveled widely and had won many honors throughout the world. Peasants and scholars alike identified him as a great man.

But there were many pressures on the great man. Analysands came to expect an almost miraculous facilitation of their individuation process. Those who had analyzed with him and moved on expected him to respond to their letters. Brilliant minds began to identify him as a worthy colleague. His work and his correspondence grew, with enormous demands on his time and energy.

On the whole Jung coped without serious difficulty. However an illness that followed a trip to India in 1937 forced him to limit some of his activities. He was sixty-two when he experienced great dis-

---

[27] See Aniela Jaffé, ed., *C.G. Jung: Word and Image.*
[28] See "Elders as Healers."

tress from dysentery. In March of that year, he wrote that this illness and the inordinate pressure of work prevented him from corresponding with others.[29] A year later he wrote to his doctor that he was doing much better, walking for three to six hours at a time, climbing mountains, working in his garden, writing "a longish paper in English" and "bursting with energy."[30] The crisis of ill health seemed to be past. Despite inner and outer pressures, Jung was once again able to give form to the creative forces that were so strong in him.

Only a year went by, however, before he wrote of "a little collapse . . . on account of overworking."[31] By that time another war was an immediate danger; Hitler was "reaching his climax and with him the German psychosis."[32] Jung wrote to M. Esther Harding in New York of "living provisionally, expecting all sorts of possibilities,"[33] hoping Switzerland would not be involved in the war.

By the spring of 1940 the threat of invasion was strong enough that Jung took the women and children of his family to refuge in the Swiss Alps near Saanen. The younger men of the family were off in the army guarding the borders of their country, now surrounded by fascist forces. Left as the only adult male in a household of women and children, transplanted from the familiarity of home and practice, Jung wrote to a friend that it felt "as if one were sitting on a box full of dynamite that might go off in the next moment. Yet one is quiet, because it is a great fatality."[34]

The stresses of exile, awaiting a war in which both his country and his loved ones might suffer, added to a feeling of impending doom. Like many who had experienced the physical and psychological devastation of the First World War, Jung had a good idea what the "fatality" of the conflict might be. Jung also felt himself under attack. Rumors that he was a Nazi caused him to write to a colleague:

---

[29] *Letters,* vol. 1, p. 232.
[30] Ibid., p. 244.
[31] Ibid., p. 271.
[32] Ibid., p. 276.
[33] Ibid.
[34] Ibid., p. 282.

I don't think that I have paranoic delusions about persecution. The difficulty is very real. Whatever I touch and wherever I go I meet with this prejudice that I'm a Nazi and that I'm in close affiliation with the German government.[35]

Allegations such as these left Jung's reputation scarred. In his role as president of the International Society for Psychotherapy, he was determined to keep the lines of communication open with its German members. He had also published an article comparing Jewish and Aryan psychologies, an article that some still interpret today as anti-Semitic.[36] While Jung did get caught in certain of the cultural stereotypes of his Victorian era, he was not anti-Semitic. He took on many Jewish analysands, some of whom became his star pupils; he also helped many Jews escape from Nazism, and encouraged one of his students to use her ties with Nazi leaders to spy for the Allies. Nevertheless, he could not seem to escape the accusation that he was pro-Nazi. That this scar remains is a reminder of how extremely difficult it is to walk the narrow line between confronting unconscious forces, within the psyche or in the outer world, and the misguided perception that one is in collaboration with those forces.

When the threat of invasion ended, Jung was able to return his family to Zürich and to spend time at Bollingen. Nevertheless, he called 1941 the *anno miseriae,* the year of misery. He felt "old and rotten," too busy with lectures, meetings and patients to write, and "very tired and deeply depressed by the senselessness of this war."[37] He was beginning to feel his age and reported, "Whenever I get a bit too tired I also feel my heart and that is decidedly disagreeable and makes me cross with the whole world."[38] Jung was then sixty-six. The misery of war intensified. Jung described the first four days after Pearl Harbor as "a period of black depression."[39]

---

[35] *Letters,* vol. 2, p. xxxiv.

[36] See "The State of Psychotherapy Today," *Civilization in Transition,* CW 10, esp. pars. 353-354.

[37] *Letters,* vol. 1, pp. 297, 299.

[38] Ibid., p. 307.

[39] Ibid.

That same month Jung responded to an inquiry about a dream:

> The valley of darkness has to be gone through in reality and not in
> fantasy, otherwise one could spare oneself an infinite number of un-
> pleasantnesses which are nevertheless important for life. I think,
> therefore, that if you keep as closely as possible to concrete reality
> and try to create yourself there and illuminate the darkness, you will
> be on a more normal road.[40]

This could have been advice to himself as well as his patient about
how to survive descent and depression. One cannot simply fantasize
an *abaissement* or the darkness of a descent. One has to know its reality, trying to find a spark of light in the blackness of unknown
forces experienced when consciousness sinks into what seems like
oblivion. The unpleasantness of inner and outer experiences that
arises at such a time cannot be avoided. It has to be lived through. As
we descend into psyche's depths, it's important to stay grounded in
the outer world as much as possible so that we keep a sense of outer
reality, even if that is painful.

Jung seemed to live out some of his advice in his own late-liminal
descent. In 1942 he gave up lecturing at the Swiss Federal Polytech-
nic in Zürich, something he had enjoyed, because he was experiencing ill health. He was intensely involved with a lecture called "The
Spirit Mercurius."[41]

> I am awfully busy on my Mercury material, and I had to live it, i.e.,
> it caught hold of me, played the transformation of Mercury on my
> own human system and gave me incidentally a remarkably miserable
> fortnight.[42]

About a week later he wrote:

> For the time being I am still immersed in Mercury, who, as he will
> always try to, has dissolved me almost and just failed to separate me
> limb from limb.[43]

---

[40] Ibid.
[41] See *Alchemical Studies,* CW 13, pars. 239-303
[42] Ibid., p. 319.
[43] Ibid., note 5.

Later he reports that he is "wrestling with this problem of the *con-iunctio* . . . . It is incredibly difficult."[44] This bore fruit in Jung's post-illness writing of his major opus, *Mysterium Coniunctionis.*[45]

In January of 1944, at age sixty-nine, Jung broke his ankle. A severe heart attack rapidly followed. His dreams and visions from this time are detailed in *Memories, Dreams, Reflections*. At one point during his illness, Jung had a series of what today are called near-death experiences. They came at the critical peak of Jung's transition into a new way of being in the world. In fact, a change in conscious attitude is frequently preceded by such a numinous experience. This was certainly true for Jung. He moved through depression and somatic response into a late-liminal *metanoia*.

In 1945, after his recovery, he wrote to a dying friend to console her and reflected on his own experience:

> Throughout my illness something has carried me. My feet were not standing on air and I had the proof that I have reached a safe ground. Whatever you do, if you do it sincerely, will eventually become the bridge to your wholeness, a good ship that carries you through the darkness of your second birth, which seems to be death to the outside. . . .
>
> Be patient and regard it as another difficult task, this time the last one.[46]

Earlier, when he was sixty-seven, Jung had written to a professional woman photographer living in Ascona:

> As one grows older one must try not to work oneself to death unnecessarily. At least that's how it is with me. . . . I can scarcely keep pace and must watch out that the creative forces do not chase me round the universe at a gallop. . . . I have to coax myself soothingly, with great assiduity and attentiveness, not to do too much.[47]

He added that on vacation at Bollingen it took him two months in order to be able to do nothing again, then continued:

---

[44] Ibid., p. 336.
[45] Ibid., note 4. *Mysterium Coniunctionis* is CW 14.
[46] Ibid., pp. 358-359.
[47] Ibid., pp. 320-321.

But as everything is the other way around with women, I presume
that your formula [for mobilizing the creative forces] is absolutely
right for the female sex. . . . To put it briefly, one might say: with
women the inner pressure must be raised with some pumped-in carbonic acid, but it is advisable for a man to fix a spigot on the barrel
so that he does not leak away completely.[48]

It is difficult for a woman in this day and age to imagine that the
recipient of such a letter wouldn't have been insulted by the pre-
sumed difference between male and female creativity. It is also difficult to imagine that Jung, who was so conscious of many of his
complexes, didn't recognize the projection of his own feminine
qualities, his anima traits, onto the actual women around him as well
as women collectively. Perhaps it was his own feminine creative
forces that needed to be energized, bubbled up, made into sparkling
water, then carefully monitored by the ego, or Self, that realized after
his severe illness that he was no longer up to being chased "round
the universe at a gallop."

Certainly the two women with whom he was most closely associ-
ated seem not to have needed "pumped-in carbonic acid" to be creative and productive. Both Emma Jung, his wife, and Toni Wolff,
his soul-partner, not only supported and encouraged him as they
aged but produced significant work of their own.

In 1942 Emma Jung was sixty. She maintained an active analytic
practice to which she had come late in life. This work had begun,
oddly enough, when one of Jung's patients dreamed that Frau Jung
had something to give her. Jung took this dream literally and encouraged his wife to begin her own practice. It's an interesting confirma-
tion of Jung's projection of the anima onto his wife that there seems
to have been no interpretation of the dream as his woman patient's
desire to receive from Jung himself the gift of his own feminine
qualities. One can only guess what those qualities might have been,
though many have written of Emma Jung's strong sensation function, as well as her patience and kindness.

---

[48] Ibid., p. 321.

Emma Jung, too, had felt the horrors of war and family upheaval. She was a fine homemaker, a good manager of her household and family. The early years of her marriage were in a country where a woman could neither vote nor have a bank account unless it was co-signed by her husband. Nevertheless, Emma Jung worked hard on her own psychological development and on her marriage. Her exchange of letters with Freud is an interesting testament to her determination to promote the growth of both her marriage and herself.[49]

Obviously hers was not an easy marriage. Most of Jung's female analysands had strong transferences to him. In other words, he became a love object for many of them. Many of them can be seen in films, taken even when Jung was an old man, gathered around him like adoring acolytes. Often Jung's countertransference was equally strong. Depth psychology involves a partnership like no other. Experiences are shared that create unbreakable bonds and a very special kind of love. Today we realize that it is abuse to act on this love. When Jung was developing his own psychology, however, little was known of the dynamics of transference and countertransference. No code of ethics had been developed. It was mostly a matter of trial and error, discovering what worked and what didn't.

The most significant of Jung's analysands proved to be Toni Wolff, who quit her own analysis with Jung at the time of his midlife crisis so that she could accompany him on his inner journey. By all accounts highly creative and intuitive, Toni had come to Jung in extreme distress. Her analytic work with Jung halted, she soon became an integral part of both the analytic group in Zürich and Jung's personal life.

A group photograph at the Weimar conference in 1911 shows Toni Wolff looking rather angry under a mass of dark curly hair, stylish and intelligent with an introverted presence that is striking in its intensity.[50] In contrast Emma Jung appears calm, beautiful, col-

---

[49] See *The Freud/Jung Letters.*

[50] A copy of this photograph appears in *Man and His Symbols*, p. 26 (but Toni Wolff is not identified).

lected in herself, as she does in most photos, never betraying any of the chaotic feelings she must have undergone finding herself in a threesome that she could not allow herself to destroy. Eventually she and Toni worked out their relationship with Jung in a creative if somewhat unorthodox fashion. It is reported that they respected one another and even worked on their dreams together, with the help of C.A. Meier, to try to prevent complexes from destroying what each had to give to Jung.[51]

Each woman had her own role and her own place in Jung's life. When Jung went to Bollingen it was often Toni who went with him. It was she who shared what Jung called his "number 2 personality," which he experienced so strongly in his tower retreat. The daily life of home, family and grounded routine was the domain of Emma. It is testimony to Emma Jung's development that she was able to say, after Toni Wolff's death, that she would always be grateful to Toni for giving Jung what she herself was unable to give.

These were some of the stresses in Emma Jung's life all through their years of marriage. The stress of living with a man of Jung's stature and drive must have had a great impact on her own individuation. Yet by the time she was fifty she had managed to do an analysis with her husband, no mean feat, and had already done significant research on one of her own passionate interests, the grail legend.

Emma was in her late fifties when the Second World War began. Little is said about how difficult this war was for her, but there must have been a great deal of pain for her in the conflict. She, too, was isolated from home and friends in Saanen. She, too, had a son and sons-in-law at the front waiting for a possible invasion of Switzerland by German forces. But even in the mountains she had to keep her household running smoothly and Jung as healthy as possible.

For most of her life a large portion of Emma's energy went into the maintenance of Jung's household in a way that made it possible for him to concentrate on his work. After her death Jung carved a stone in her honor on which he lettered in Chinese symbols, "She

---

[51] See Suzanne Wagner, *Matter of Heart*, p. 16.

was the foundation of my house."[52] During her croning years she actively worked as an analyst and teacher. She was also involved in the development of the Analytical Psychology Club of Zürich. Later, after the Zürich Institute was founded in 1948, she was a member of the Curatorium, a role she took very seriously and to which she devoted a great deal of time.

With all of these responsibilities, she still managed to leave a significant body of work after her death: her essays published as *Animus and Anima,* and the unfinished grail material, later compiled and edited by Marie-Louise von Franz. These works are valuable sources for both men and women, especially those coming to age. For those of us going through the trials of a late-liminal transition her psychological amplification of the struggles of Perceval in the grail legend can be particularly helpful. As we read about his trials, we can perceive the opportunities we, ourselves, have missed through our own unconsciousness as we try to find a way back to balance at the center, symbolized by the grail.

Laurens van der Post saw Toni Wolff as a Bernese aristocrat of great intelligence. She was a person of substance who bubbled with energy that showed in everything from her intense manner of smoking, driving and listening, to her work as an analyst and writer. Van der Post describes her as a "person whose thinking and intuitive functions were superior attributes," and as "Jung's most intimate companion and guide during those long, protracted years of his critical encounter with the blind forces of [the] collective unconscious."[53] Jung's relationship with Toni lasted from before those First World War years until her death in 1953 at age sixty-five.

It appears that for most of her adult life Toni Wolff carried the projection of Jung's "hetaira" anima, making it possible for him to know that aspect of himself more fully through knowing her. In her essay "Structural Forms of the Feminine Psyche," Wolff describes a four-fold model of women's typology: mother, hetaira, amazon and me-

---

52 See Laurens Van der Post, *Jung and the Story of Our Time,* p. 177.
53 Ibid., p. 175.

dial woman.[54] The hetaira functions to awaken the individual psychic life of others. This, from all accounts, is the role she played in Jung's life. Jung told Van der Post that he wished, after her death, to carve a stone for her with a Chinese character meaning that she was the "fragrance" of his house.[55]

At the time of Toni's death Jung was seventy-eight and Emma seventy-one. For many years Toni was known to the outside world chiefly as the "other woman" in Jung's life. Only in recent years has it become more and more clear that she managed to do her own work even as she supported Jung in his. Friends and colleagues have written of her strength, presenting a picture of her as a remarkably intelligent and psychologically strong human being.[56] C.A. Meier, the analyst with whom she and Emma worked, preserved much of her writing "so that her distinguished record in this regard [could be] secure and her own psychological achievement [made available] to be studied and used."[57] According to Barbara Hannah, Jung saw her as a gifted writer and was disappointed that she spent her time with patients and developing the Psychology Club of Zürich instead of writing.[58] Her relationship with Jung must have imposed a great burden on her, for she had to repress the natural desire to force him into a choice between his wife and her.

Emma and Toni understood that he needed them both and that the loss of either would be detrimental to his life and work. Emma at least had society's approval of her role. Toni had only the support of those who knew and understood the importance of her decision to stay in the triangle. Of course this disparity took a toll on Toni both

---

[54] For an outline and discussion of her model, see Donald Lee Williams, *Border Crossings: A Psychological Perspective on Carlos Castaneda's Path of Knowledge,* pp. 119-121.

[55] *Jung and the Story of Our Time,* p. 177.

[56] See Barbara Hannah, *Jung: His Life and Work: A Biographical Memoir,* as well as the biographies written by Van der Post and von Franz.

[57] Van der Post, *Jung and the Story of Our Time,* pp. 170-171. (Toni Wolff's collected papers are currently being translated for publication in English.)

[58] *Jung: His Life and Work,* p. 149.

psychologically and physically. Her own transition in the croning years was into death that happened quite swiftly and unexpectedly in 1953. She saw an analysand on the afternoon of the night on which she died.

Jung himself almost died in his late-liminal transition. His heart attack precipitated visions of a mystic marriage that filled the room with such radiance that he feared for the lives of any who entered. Myths tell us over and over again that those who experience the radiance of the gods are often burned to cinders by the experience. Jung survived, but when he wrote about the illness he said that he would not last much longer: "I am marked. But life has fortunately become provisional. It has become a transitory prejudice, a working hypothesis for the time being, but not existence itself."[59]

Jung was not yet seventy. He lived fifteen years more. Much of his most important thinking and writing took place during those late years—*Aion, Mysterium Coniunctionis* and *Alchemical Studies,* for example. He had survived the deaths of the two women he loved most; Toni Wolff when he was seventy-eight, Emma when he was eighty. If he lived provisionally, he nevertheless lived fully, with the legacy of those years as testimony to the creativity that can follow one's transition into age. In *Memories, Dreams, Reflections* he wrote of his late-liminal crisis and *metanoia:*

> After the illness a fruitful period of work began for me. A good many of my principal works were written only then. The insight I had had, or the vision of the end of all things, gave me the courage to undertake new formulations. I no longer attempted to put across my own opinion, but surrendered myself to the current of my thoughts. Thus one problem after the other revealed itself to me and took shape.[60]

But something else came to him as a result of his illness—"an affirmation of things as they are: an unconditional 'yes' to that which is."[61] He felt a new acceptance of the conditions of existence, includ-

---

[59] *Letters,* vol. 1, p. 359.
[60] *Memories, Dreams, Reflections,* p. 297.
[61] Ibid.

ing acceptance of his own nature, just as he was.

> At the beginning of the illness I had the feeling that there was something wrong with my attitude, and that I was to some extent responsible for the mishap. But when one follows the path of individuation, when one lives one's own life, one must take mistakes into the bargain; life would not be complete without them.[62]

In 1946 Jung wrote to an American writer on psychology:

> Not very long ago I recognized the immense truth of being the *hsiao jên* [literally "the little man," the common man]. . . . Only the *hsiao jên* contains the *chên-jên* [the true, or perfect man].[63]

But even with this revelation Jung's trials were not over. In the fall of 1946 Jung had another heart attack, this time a very serious embolism. That December he reported to Victor White, an English Dominican priest with whom he had a strong late-life friendship, that he had had a marvelous dream:

> One bluish diamond, like a star high in heaven, reflected in a round quiet pool—heaven above, heaven below. The *imago Dei* [God image] in the darkness of the earth, this is myself. The dream meant a great consolation. I am no more a black and endless sea of misery and suffering but a certain amount thereof contained in a divine vessel. . . . I confess I am afraid of a long drawn-out suffering. It seems to me as if I am ready to die, although as it looks to me some powerful thoughts are still flickering like lightnings in a summer night. Yet they are not mine, they belong to God, as [does] everything else which bears mentioning.[64]

Apparently the ego-Self axis, the relationship between the "small man" and the "true man," had changed profoundly. Jung's creative thoughts, like "flickering lightnings," were coming not from ego but from a deeper source of wisdom. This wisdom is evident in the book *Aion* that Jung began writing in December, 1947. He describes its inception in this way:

---

[62] Ibid.

[63] *Letters,* vol. 1, p. 426.

[64] Ibid., p. 450.

I simply had to write a new essay I did not know about what. . . . I was against it, because I wanted to rest my head. . . . In spite of everything, I felt forced to write on blindly, not seeing at all what I was driving at. Only after I had written about 25 pages in folio, it began to dawn on me that Christ—not the man but the divine being—was my secret goal. It came to me as a shock, as I felt utterly unequal to such a task.[65]

After the publication of *Aion,*[66] Jung continued to work and to write. Creativity may not have chased him around at a gallop, but it never ceased to move him. Though forced to limit his practice, he continued to see patients and to maintain his friendships through meetings and letters. He also supervised an addition to his tower and worked with stone.

At age seventy-five he carved the now famous Bollingen stone,[67] the cornerstone that had literally been rejected by the builders of his addition. On one face of the stone he carved a circle, and in it a *kabir,* a tiny homunculus with lantern in hand. In the circle around it he carved a Greek inscription that translates:

Time is a child—playing like a child—playing a board game—the kingdom of the child. This is Telesphoros, who roams through the dark regions of this cosmos and glows like a star out of the depths. He points the way to the gates of the sun and to the land of dreams.[68]

On the third face he inscribed an alchemical saying:

I am an orphan, alone; nevertheless I am found everywhere. I am one, but opposed to myself. I am youth and old man at one and the same time. I have known neither father nor mother, because I have had to be fetched out of the deep like a fish, or fell like a white stone from heaven. In woods and mountains I roam, but I am hidden in the innermost soul of man. I am mortal for everyone, yet I am not touched by the cycle of aeons.[69]

---

[65] Ibid., p. 480.
[66] CW 9ii.
[67] Pictured in Aniela Jaffé, ed., *C.G. Jung: Word and Image,* pp. 204-205.
[68] *Memories, Dreams, Reflections,* p. 227.
[69] Ibid.

In alchemy the stone that is despised and rejected is the Philosophers' Stone, the "orphan," a symbol of the Self and of the inner gold we try, through individuation, to transmute from the base metals of our very human *hsiao jên* lives. In this context it is moving to read in von Franz's biography of Jung:

> A couple of years ago the son of a stone mason from the neighborhood [of Jung's tower] said to me: "These days masons don't know how to work with natural stone any more. But old Jung, down there by the lake, he knew all right. He knew the right way to take a stone in your hand."[70]

It seems that Jung took into his hand many raw unworked stones, large and small, real and metaphorical.

It is reported that the Inuit meditate on each stone or tusk they intend to work until its reality begins to emerge in their mind and soul. Only then do they pick up a tool. Alistair MacDuff writes:

> The Eskimo carver . . . takes his time in considering a selected piece of stone, and if it happens to be a choice piece, he will spend a very long time studying it, sometimes several months, allowing his thoughts to fully crystallize before he approaches his tools. . . . From previous experience of a given area or strata of stone, he will know what to expect of the colours inherent in it after polishing.[71]

In a similar fashion Jung worked with his patients and with himself, releasing the colors of the personality. He was frequently aided by the two women who were closest to him. They chose to do this, but not without the cost of pain and turmoil as they struggled to work through their relationships to Jung and to each other as well as to their patients and their work. At the same time they were true to themselves, and in the end we see that both women left their own creative mark, worked their own stone. While it is not as easy to identify *metanoia* in their late-liminal years as it is in Jung's, we can identify the strains they endured and recognize their creative output. We know that Jung did indeed undergo profound crises during his

---

[70] *C.G. Jung: His Myth in Our Time,* p. 234, footnote.
[71] *Lords of the Stone,* p. 23.

sixties and early seventies and that these upheavals of body and psyche enabled, perhaps even forced, him to give unrestricted voice to the Self.

In his last years, after a period of doubt about the project, apparently still having difficulty seeing himself as more than a *hsiao jên,* hardly worth memorializing, Jung accepted Aniela Jaffé's assistance in writing his autobiography. His "Late Thoughts" are a goldmine of elder wisom. Here is one:

> It was only after the illness [in 1944] that I understood how important it is to affirm one's own destiny. In this way we forge an ego that does not break down when incomprehensible things happen; an ego that endures, that endures the truth, and that is capable of coping with the world and with fate. Then, to experience defeat is also to experience victory. Nothing is disturbed—neither inwardly nor outwardly, for one's own continuity has withstood the current of life and of time. But that can come to pass only when one does not meddle inquisitively with the workings of fate.[72]

The challenge of incomprehensible things happening may come to any of us. Hopefully, especially as we go through our croning years, we too may reach a place where we experience victory in our defeats. To accept ourselves and our lives as they are is a lesson we would all like to learn. That and developing an ego that endures the truth and does not meddle with fate, seem to be goals we all strive for as we go through the transitional passage of coming to age.

---

[72] *Memories, Dreams, Reflections,* p. 297.

3

Transitional Passages

We long for meaning and growth in our croning years. But in a culture of fast food, fast cars and fast action there is little space or tolerance for the slow ripening of coming to age. Instead of affirming gray hair, slowed reflexes or the inner wisdom of life experience, we are bombarded by instructions to deny and hide our years. Ads arrive daily at our doors advising, "There's no need to grow old," "Fifteen ways to stay young," "Aging can be stopped!"

How, then, do we learn to accept and negotiate this crucial life stage in a positive way? Can we, like Jung and his followers, carry on through the struggles of loss, illness or depression and emerge with new strength? Can we find our own individual ways through initiation into age?

Confucius is reputed to have said that only after sixty could one be wise enough to study books of ancient wisdom. Before that age even the wisest are too green to understand. Primitive shamen seem to agree. Joan Halifax tells us that most medicine men are in their late-liminal years before they consider themselves shamen. She reports that she has never known a true shaman under the age of sixty-five. Until then the rigors of training often bring so much pain and suffering that the initiate has little energy for ordinary life. This is the shaman's path that eventually leads to an integration of body, mind and spirit beyond what most of us in more "civilized" cultures have ever experienced. Halifax remarks on "the archetypal humor" of these people as well as their humility and psychological openness.[73]

In our modern society we tend to deny suffering as a way to integrity. We also deny age. Yet both are important teachers. They impart a tensile strength to the personality so that we bend rather than

---

[73] "Elders as Healers."

break when tested. If we believe the media ads promoting age-masking and youth-restoring products, trendy diets and skin rejuvenators, we're apt to forget the importance of aging and of pain. In tribal cultures old ones are sought out for advice and counsel. They are the wise ones who can see beyond the surface because they have experienced the depths. They are the keepers of cultural traditions, the ones who tell the medicine stories, the ones who can guide because they have been there themselves. In contrast, the elders of our culture are seen as objects of pity rather than as guides and teachers.

Today few of us believe that there is such a thing as a wise old man or woman. We see them as powerful psychological images, but dismiss them in our lives as fantasies with no outer reality. Primitives believed that when the menses ceased in older women it was because the "wise blood" had backed up to be held in the womb where it would create a new way of being.[74] Today such a concept is considered laughably naive. Few see its psychological meaning: wisdom birthing from an aging psyche, just as children are born from a younger womb. Likewise we denigrate the alchemical concept of the old man with the wind in his belly, gestating a new being.

We teach our young that when an object begins to show wear or break down it should be discarded and replaced. Our environment is filled with the debris of such a philosophy. Can we accept such conspicuous consumption of people as well? Even the elders in Western society resist the idea of value and wisdom in age. Men struggle to maintain a macho attitude. Women struggle to look young. In a culture where a youthful persona—face, body and style—are the supreme values, these struggles seem like necessities. They may save us from the inflation of identifying with the archetype of the wise old man or woman, but they rob us of access to the wisdom, creativity and power of natural aging.

Once upon a time, the wise old woman was called a crone. She was honored by her people because she knew how to heal and could

---

[74] See Barbara Walker, *The Crone: Woman of Age, Wisdom, and Power,* p. 52.

see through to the true meaning of events. Today, after centuries of denigration and persecution, she is perceived as a parody, a figure of ridicule, a hag who fattens children up to eat them. Today older women often see themselves as this kind of crone. Only the young are desirable, trustworthy, productive.

Barbara Walker points out that women in our society are not allowed to age normally through their full life cycle, but instead are constrained to create an illusion that their aging stops in their twenties or thirties. She also makes the interesting observation that older women are made invisible through others' refusal to see them. For instance they are rarely seen on movie or television screens. "Women are socially and professionally handicapped by wrinkles and gray hair," she writes. "A multi-billion dollar 'beauty' industry exploits women's well-founded fear of looking old."[75]

Body appearance does take on an exaggerated importance for many aging people in our society. They notice every wrinkle, every age spot, each tiny sign of deterioration. Postmenopausal women, while relieved of the stress of menstruation, often find themselves avoiding mirrors because the person who looks back seems a stranger. Feeling like the same person, one is suddenly surprised to see a body so different. Men too are expected never to sag, to keep their hair and their erections.

As we age we do need to pay more attention to our weight, diet and exercise. We can too easily become complacent about these things when we no longer feel the need to be objects of desire. When we see failing health and physical loss as inevitable components of the aging process, the temptation is to let our bodies and psyches go, to stop taking responsibility for our mental and physical welfare.

Alice did just that. After retirement she lived alone. She stopped eating meals because it was too lonely to eat by herself. She stopped dressing most days, because there was no place to go and no one to see her. As her appearance deteriorated it became more and more difficult for her to go out even to shop. Only when a friend inter-

---

[75] Ibid., p. 59.

vened and Alice was hospitalized did she begin to recover and take responsibility for her health and her life. Only when she had joined in the programs at a center for retired persons, where she made friends, did she begin to think again about her appearance and take care of her hair and her clothing.

Even when one does care, the physical changes that come with age can be a shock. Dee, a highly successful and intelligent fifty-nine-year-old executive, reported the shock of seeing herself caught in an unguarded moment on home video. She was horrified at what she saw as a parody of her former self. "I looked old," she protested. "Old and stupid and demented."

There is a prevalent perception today that older people do look stupid and demented. This is not a conscious attitude but comes from a powerful unconscious collective constellation that possesses us when we let our guard down. What Jung called the shadow, those undesired traits that we've repressed and locked up within ourselves, joins with other unconscious parts of ourselves that we haven't yet consciously integrated (like an opinionated animus or a moody anima) to create certain attitudes and prejudices.

Often we project our own undesirable qualities onto others. If we are old, for example, we may see the young as thoughtless, promiscuous, drug addicted and living on the edge, never realizing that we have projected these qualities of carelessness and rebellion rather than acknowledging their presence in our own psyches. We may develop strong opinions against such traits in the young. "This could never have happened in MY day!" Or we may get depressed and fall into a sour mood. "When I look at the young people of today and see how irresponsible they are, I feel utterly hopeless." On the other hand, those who are young may see us as stodgy, conservative and resistant to change, unaware of the same traits in themselves.

Maturity may help us to differentiate ourselves from the projections of those who reward youth and denigrate age, but when such voices and attitudes attack us from within, our view of ourselves may become as distorted and twisted as the very words used to describe us: witch, hag, biddy, dodderer, old fart, prune. Under such an internal barrage most of us can barely intuit the possibility of creativity or psychological rebirth. Instead we would abort every aspect of age. Even death sometimes seems preferable to getting old.

At the same time as these self-demeaning attitudes have us in their grip, the average life span is lengthening. Daniel Callahan of the Hastings Center tells us that by the year 2050, American women will have an average life expectancy of 83.6 years and men 79.8.[76] In fact, he projects that in another 65 years the average life span at birth could easily be 100. If this is true, it seems likely that the years of coming to age will also increase. Therefore, isn't it vital that we try to develop some guidelines to help people make the transition into age a time of full living rather than of giving up? How, then, do we begin to perceive ourselves more realistically at fifty, sixty or seventy as still valuable to ourselves and to society?

The quest for understanding of this time of life has led me to studies in gerontology as well as to Jungian psychology. Experience with dreams, sandplay, mythology and the analysis of older people has provided some guidelines for my work as an analyst. What the process of coming to age entails is still open to speculation and discovery. My hope is that others will also begin to plow these fields.

The late-liminal period of life brings changes in body and circumstances that signal a new beginning. If one is to be in the world in a new and creative way, one must accept both the tasks and the challenges presented by these alterations. The signs of a new beginning are recognizable. They are both outer and inner. One may appear childish at times, as we often experience regression before a big move forward. This may be falsely diagnosed as pathological unless seen in context. Many people at this time of life fear that they are suffering from early senile dementia because they are forgetful, disoriented, depressed and physically ill. They can't find their house keys, they forget important engagements, they go to another room to get something and can't remember what they went for. The familiar world around them also seems subtly changed. They may not quite

---

[76] *Setting Limits: Medical Goals in an Aging Society,* p. 226.

recognize themselves. Often they feel like the old woman in the English folk song who awakened from sleep on the roadside to find her petticoats had been cut off at the knees by a passing tramp. "Lackamercy me, this is none of I!" she exclaimed over and over again. Even her old dog didn't recognize her and tried to chase her out of the yard when she returned home.

When we find ourselves in a liminal time/space vestibule between one way of being and another, our conscious energy is apt to disappear into the unconscious and become unavailable to us in our daily life. It is as if we fell asleep on the road to age. When this happens, we may feel as if we've suddenly lost pieces of ourselves. Our persona, the way we "clothe" ourselves in public, may become damaged. Then we are unfamiliar even to our instinctual selves (the dog). We feel out of sorts, wondering who we have become. "I don't know who I am anymore!" wailed one woman in analysis. It is a hard task to bear the loss of one's old identity while waiting for the new to emerge.

Loss of the old persona often makes older people feel invisible. One aging woman told Florida Scott-Maxwell that she was sure she could walk in and out of any house virtually unobserved.[77] In a younger person this feeling of not being seen or acknowledged might be taken as a sign of pathology. In someone older it is often based on the actual responses of others as well as on feelings of having lost oneself in the borderlands between conscious and unconscious, between what has been and what is to come, between the harvest and the winter of life.

Anamnesis is the re-membering of one's life events, family, friends, significant times and places, giving them order and new meaning. Such remembering seems to ease the difficulty of staying in that borderland. It is my experience that the body carries many memories in its cells and that their release can be facilitated and greatly enriched by hands-on body work with a trained professional and by working imaginatively with the body in analysis. Descent into

---

[77] "We Are the Sum of Our Days," p. 3.

the body and release of old "matters" can be managed consciously or fallen into unconsciously. It seems almost inevitable that one must "go unconscious" in some way if transformation is to happen. This is part of any initiation. I agree with Jung that "anyone who is destined to descend into a deep pit had better set about it with all necessary precautions rather than risk failing into the hole backwards."[78]

We often experience such a descent as loss of verve in our outer lives. It's as if the energy previously available to the demands of daily living were suddenly withdrawn and invested in a growth fund in the unconscious. This is seldom a conscious decision. We don't usually say, "Now I'm going to put my energy into the unconscious," or "I've decided to individuate." Something happens beyond our control and we find ourselves in a state of ennui. The simplest tasks seem monumental. This may last a day or it may last much longer. In some instances the depletion of energy can last for months or even years, as the work goes on in the unconscious.

This work, obviously, isn't only mental. Our whole being is involved—mind, body and spirit—sometimes in a painful and even life-threatening fashion. Somatizing (translating psychic content into physical symptom) may play an especially important part in the process of change, as it did in Jung's late-liminal transition. The writing Jung did in his seventies and eighties might not have been possible without the experiences he went through after his heart attack. Recognizing somatic symptoms as symbols of initiation aids the process of transformation.

There are times when it takes all one's moral fiber to simply hang in and continue to live as one or another debilitating disease invades the body. Frequently these are organically based and must be accepted as such. For example, we may be suffering emotionally from a broken heart, but if this manifests as a heart attack it probably won't be healed with psychological work alone. Somatic symptoms are physically real and often require physical remedies. It may be part of our late-liminal taks to deal with illness. As we age, the defenses

---

[78] *Aion*, CW 9ii, par. 125.

of the immune system are apt to weaken. The ability of the hypothalamus to differentiate between cells that belong to our physical organ-
ism and those that don't may decrease. When physical weakening is
accompanied by an inability to differentiate between the cells that are
"me" and those that are "not-me," we are apt to get caught in the unconscious, where it becomes more and more difficult to sort out what
belongs to us and what to others. It's as if our personality begins to
dissolve into the mass.

When somatization is part of our lives it's hard to keep an intact
sense of ourselves. Metaphorically we are in the pot cooking, or in
the fire tempering, or in the depths of a cave or the sea searching for
treasure—all common dream motifs. We may be reminded of our
physicality by body aches or by more serious symptoms. While it is
tempting to see these only in a negative light, it's also important to
realize that they keep us grounded in our own bodies and our own
lives at the same time that we are undergoing a psychological dissolution.

When these things happen, we may try to cling to old attitudes that
harden into saturnine rigidity, expressed in sour opinions and stiffen-
ing joints. Acknowledging this as a defense against change, the task
is to find ways to let go, to accept and allow the slow and often
painful transformation of our bodies, our conscious attitudes and our
souls. Often this means letting go of the heroic attitudes we worked
so hard to develop earlier in life, recognizing that these have either
lost their meaning or been temporarily taken from us. They, too,
must be transformed.

As we face up to the losses of coming to age, we may become
more and more aware of the downward pull into a late-life *abaissement du niveau mentale*, a lowering of the level of consciousness to a
point where the ego seems to be possessed by forces over which
even the strongest or most mature personality has little control. As
Jung writes:

> *[Abaissement]* is a slackening of the tensity of consciousness, which
> might be compared to a low barometric reading, presaging bad
> weather. The tonus has given way, and this is felt subjectively as

listlessness, moroseness, and depression. One no longer has any wish or courage to face the tasks of the day. One feels like lead, because no part of one's body seems willing to move, and this is due to the fact that one no longer has any disposable energy.[79]

Claire, recently retired from a meaningful and successful career, despaired: "I really have no reason to get up in the morning anymore. I try to get involved in life, in all the retirement plans I made, but then my body rebels and the first thing I know I'm back in bed feeling miserable and crazy and sick again."

While in analysis, Claire had experienced a life-threatening illness followed by the death of her mother with whom she still had a symbiotic tie. These events plus her retirement triggered a profound depression. Her spouse was going through a similar crisis and was unable to give her the support she craved. Claire felt abandoned, hopeless and unbearably lonely. The *abaissement* she was experiencing had all the signs of regression and descent.

Soon after starting analysis Claire had to be hospitalized again, after which she spent a long time going from doctor to doctor, searching for a cure. While she was able to keep herself and her house in some semblance of order, nothing alleviated the angst at the deepest levels of her being. To her bewilderment what she identified as her long mourning for her mother just kept deepening. She had dreams of falling down, unable to get up, or sitting at an empty table waiting for food that never came. She was frequently incapacitated by her illness yet always managed to keep her analytic appointments.

Listening to her I often found myself overwhelmed, struggling to stay awake in our sessions, drawn down by an overpowering pull into the unconscious. At first I told myself it was the late afternoon hour, or my identification with some of her physical symptoms, or my own lack of sleep. Strong coffee, change to an earlier hour, even secretly pinching myself, didn't change things at all. We were going down together.

---

[79] "Concerning Rebirth," *The Archetypes and the Collective Unconscious,* CW 9i, pars. 213f.

Then one day I began to notice something strange and new in my response to her. I suddenly saw that I had spontaneously assumed a posture where my arms were held as if cuddling and rocking a baby. As I held this image in my imagination in one session after another, I noticed that sometimes my breasts felt full. At the same time I began to feel a deep sense of admiration and affection for the courage it took for Claire just to get out of bed every morning. I began to look forward to her visits and to care deeply about each little event in her life: each trip to the doctor, each interaction with her spouse, each memory of her mother. Her dreams began to get richer—or at least my perception of them was enriched.

This development of a positive mother-child relationship showed in my feeling and acting the part of the good mother (countertransference) in response to Claire perceiving me and treating me as if I were (transference). Slowly I began to realize that we were now working at very early childhood developmental levels in which I had become the container for her reworking of herself and her life, starting in the preverbal years. At first it was difficult to accept that Claire could walk into my office as a sixty-year-old woman, one who had overcome many obstacles to create a career and a home and a fairly stable ego, who at the same time was experiencing herself as an infant who needed to be imaginally held and mirrored.

Why was such a regression necessary at age sixty, and what did it have to do with late-life development? What did it mean that I began to relate to this woman as if she were a baby? To try to make some sense of this, I reread Jung's work on the child.

Jung wrote of the connection between the preverbal baby and the "child" of the future personality in "The Psychology of the Child Archetype."[80] When I read it something fell into place. I began to realize that only as the wounded baby of our past is given attention can the new "child" of a fruitful old age come into being. I also began to appreciate firsthand, seeing it clearly in my hours with Claire, how important is the work of early childhood development theorists (like

---

[80] Ibid., par. 278.

Klein, Guntrip and Winnicott, initiators of object relations theory) to the analyst who works with an aging population, where so often the relationship to the mother, whether personal or archetypal, has in some way been lost, along with a part of the personality.

It now seems to me that all of us, as we come to age, are called to answer this question: Who is the child of our future development who we somehow lost, abandoned or never knew in earlier life?

Elaine, a writer in her late sixties, brought me a story she had written soon after college in which the "other" of herself was locked away in an attic. Through a crack in the wall her imprisoned self could see the outer figure she had become, going through all the stages of her life, "while the real me was locked up!" In analysis a mystic side of herself that Elaine had literally locked up since early childhood began to emerge and be acknowledged.

This part of her personality, dismissed by a pragmatic environment, had lived for the better part of sixty years in the unconscious, much as anchoresses (mystic nuns) lived sequestered in huts at the center of medieval villages, watching the action but keeping silence. Elaine began to read about anchoresses and their overseeing of children's play and community affairs even as they remained in a state of prayer. Slowly, over a period of time, she began to accept her own strong spiritual side, realizing that it did not have to be repressed in order to avoid conflict with a practical engagement in life.

Many of us know the feeling of having abandoned some part of ourselves as we've journeyed through life. Perhaps this is one reason why, as we go through late-liminal transitions, we feel so cut off from the outer collective and so invisible. Could it be that we are separated from our own authenticity?

Even those with very strong egos frequently find themselves in a bewildered state, with fears of senility or Alzheimer's lurking in the shadows. Lost parts of our personalities call us once again into our bodies, into our souls, often deeper into the unconscious than we've ever been. One image for such a descent is that of spiraling around all the circles within the tree of life to get to our core. The older we are, the more rings in the spiral. Others speak of a dissolution, feeling that their former ego stance is no longer firm. "I feel like jello," one analysand reported, "all jiggly and melting down."

When an experience of this kind happens, we may begin to notice an ego split. While the mute, dark, formless chaos of preverbal archetypal depths draws one's familiar sense of self (ego) into a most profound regression, typically experienced as a debilitating depression, the functioning ego developed over the course of a lifetime continues the daily tasks of life. This is not done without difficulty, but it happens, especially in later years.

The work of late-life individuation is never quite what we anticipate. It is similar to midlife work but also entirely different. It is common to all yet highly individual. It is soul work, body work, complex work. It is child work and it is adult work. Yet who but ourselves can tell us how to find our authenticity? And who can tell us how to come to age?

Contemporary men and women have few role models for aging. Without a companion the journey through late-liminal depths can be dark, lonely and frightening. No wonder many turn back, even when the alternative is rigidity, pain and retreat into what D.W. Winnicott terms the "false self."[81] But if this is our vocation, there is no choice but to go into and through the late-liminal miasma. If we can endure, we may eventually emerge with a new vision of our future. We may even experience what Jung called the transcendent function, which works to bridge the opposites within the psyche.

Elaine, for instance, wrote sensible and scientific pieces for intellectual journals. She had little if any spiritual life until her dreams and longings pointed her back to the revealing story she had written in her youth. Rediscovering and understanding its message was like recovering a piece of herself very different from her ego personality. She was reminded of her forgotten story at just the right moment. Something beyond intellect or intuition connected the opposites in a way that enriched her life. That something, it would seem, was an example of what Jung meant:

---

81 See "Ego Distortions in Terms of True and False Self."

The tendencies of the conscious and the unconscious are the two factors that together make up the transcendent function. It is called "transcendent" because it makes the transition from one attitude to another organically possible.[82]

When we are called to *metanoia*, we are called to creativity and to a new awareness. Underlying and infusing this late-liminal time is a most exciting and demanding task: that of re-imagining ourselves, of journeying beyond our present limitations so that we may welcome the spark of a new consciousness as it slowly emerges from our deepest darkness. Most of us don't know yet what such experiences of coming to age will bring. What does it mean to he a crone? How do we cross this threshold and enter a new phase of our lives? Who can give us the answers?

The truth, of course, is that the answers must come from within, from our own dreams and experiences, from our bodies and the mysteries they hold. But we can also learn from the voices of those who have explored aging in other ways, the subject of the next chapter. Thus we may come to know ourselves better and have an idea of what to expect in both the disintegration that precedes *metanoia* and the reintegration that follows.

---

[82] "The Transcendent Function," *The Structure and Dynamics of the Psyche,* CW 8, par. 145.

4

Other Voices

In the past, life in Western society generally followed expected patterns. For the average worker, retirement came at around sixty-five. By that time children were grown and grandchildren were in college or the work force. Often the retired person moved in with family members who could take care of him or her as health or financial resources failed. It has become increasingly apparent in recent years, however, that this model no longer suits the needs of the present aging generation in which the majority is still vital and independent in their sixties and even seventies. Why, then, do so many of us feel guilty when we can't follow such an outdated paradigm?

Many voices speak of *old* age, fewer of the years that precede it. Often, however, in speaking of the truly old, gerontologists and psychologists inform our croning years as well. These theorists offer insights about life stages that can be extremely helpful. Voices that speak directly to the transitional years between fifty and seventy are apt to be those of writers and analysands. Their stories and myths can inform our attitudes toward aging at a level of psyche below consciousness but at times profoundly important.[83] We need voices that speak to the soul, perhaps even more than those that speak to the intellect. One of the beauties of myths, stories and dreams is that they resonate in the unconscious complexes that influence our conscious attitudes. We shall examine some of these visions in later pages.

But first we will look at some theories of aging. Three that to me seem particularly applicable to the late-liminal years are the developmental, the activity and the disengagement theories.

Developmental theory sees life as a series of stages, starting at

---

[83] Erich Neumann believes that a change in the conscious attitude doesn't amount to much unless accompanied by changes in the unconscious components of the personality. See *Art and the Creative Unconscious*, p. 151.

birth. It holds that a noticeable shift occurs each time one enters a new stage and that each stage presents us with its own developmental tasks. Activity theory counsels one to stay active and maintain one's familiar life style as long as possible. Disengagement theory, on the other hand, believes that the slowing down of age is almost a relief, because it allows one to withdraw somewhat from outer activity and gain more time for introspection. Each of these theories has something to offer a Jungian approach to aging.

In *Childhood and Society,* Erik Erikson, one of the well-known developmental theorists, describes eight basic stages of human development. The first six apply to childhood and early adulthood, making it appear that his theory is not applicable to the late-liminal years. Yet if we look at each stage he describes as holding a particular kind of potential for a person coming to age, then we can apply his entire model to the croning years as well. If we see the child of whom he speaks as something developing within the psyche of the older adult rather than as a literal infant, we can learn quite a lot about the stages we may go through in our later years.

Stage One Erikson calls "Trust vs. Basic Mistrust." A baby needs to overcome mistrust in favor of a basic trust that then gives drive and hope to its life. The first step in accepting a future as we age is trust that no matter what happens we will somehow manage to cope with age, be tempered by it, find meaning in it, whether what lies ahead be health or illness, wealth or poverty, life or death. This means that we must overcome a basic mistrust in our own future and the future of the world.

Stage Two Erikson calls "Autonomy vs. Shame and Doubt." Maturing enough to release or retain bowel movements, the child develops either control and pride over its own production or shame and doubt about it. For a baby, a bowel movement is its first creative output. The creative output of persons in the croning years—painting, writing, cooking, gardening, for example—frequently produces pride in the excellence of one's achievement. Conversely, a lack of production or disappointment in the final product can produce shame and doubt. Some take great pride in creative work. Others denigrate their efforts. Even when praised they say, "Oh, it's not much." Often they hide or destroy their work because it doesn't meet some inner standard. Or they stop doing it at all, thus retaining the creative product rather than releasing it. Perhaps physical constipation and creative constipation are not so very different. To remedy either we need more fiber!

In Erikson's Stage Three, "Initiative vs. Guilt," the child is walking and has developed an awareness of his or her own genitalia. In a boy this means "phallic-intrusive" modes of behavior. In a girl it means "catching," by being either aggressively snatching or attractive and endearing.

It was one of Jung's insights that aging often brings the development of gender qualities within an individual that have previously been less conscious and therefore less developed. For women who have not already developed masculine characteristics, their assertiveness or phallic thrust sometimes appears like that of a little boy. For older men, a "bitchy" aggressive snatching or the attractive and endearing charm of a little girl may appear. In either gender these new qualities often show up as aggression, jealousy, rivalry, manipulation and bitterness; in other words, as inferior feelings or behaviors leading to guilt that boundaries may have been transgressed. They may be boundaries set by society or outdated but still powerful internalized parental attitudes. For example a woman who assertively speaks out at a town meeting goes and cries in the bathroom because she is sure she has transgressed the rules and made a fool of herself. A man who discovers how much he loves to cook, and care for and charm his grandchildren, doesn't tell his friends because he thinks he has to maintain a strong, macho persona in order to be respected.

Erikson's Stage Four, "Industry vs. Inferiority," is a time of work and learning to become a provider. The child learns to win recognition by producing things. But when life fails to maintain a child's gains in earlier stages, development is disrupted. When capabilities include the needed skills, one learns the pleasure of a job well done and moves toward becoming a productive member of society. Similarly, with programs like Elder Hostel and Senior Citizen Centers, many of us are still in school of one kind or another where we do experience the pleasure of a job well done. At an inner level, however, the child of our developing future may feel inadequate and inferior, because society gives this child little affirmation. Then we ourselves need to affirm our developing personalities, for as Jung wrote, they show in the autumn what the spring has engendered.[84]

In Stage Five, "Identity vs. Role Diffusion," as one matures sexually, childhood proper comes to an end. This leads either to a strong sense of identity or to doubts about one's sexuality and place in the world. Erikson believes that puberty rites help to integrate the new identity. If the child of our undeveloped gender matures, do we once again have doubts about our sexuality and our place in the world? Women may find themselves attracted to other women, and men to other men. Do we see this as normal development or as an aberration? We are developing a new identity as the child of our age matures. This may lead to all sorts of surprising changes, not only in our sexual orientation but also in our sense of place in the world.

Only after a person has mastered these five stages is it possible, according to Erikson, to begin to master the Sixth Stage, that of "Intimacy vs. Isolation." Here there is an ability to lose oneself in the meeting of bodies and minds, leading to a gradual expansion of ego interests and a connection with others. For some of us coming to age, this joining may be physical; for others it is psychological. Many older individuating persons, however, experience themselves as part of a whole much larger than their individual ego, sensing a meeting and joining with that higher power, the Self.

The awareness of oneself as a part of something much larger can bring the profound change in attitude that we have already called *metanoia*. One is then both more and less involved in affairs of the world. Friendship, children, daily tasks begin to seem more attractive than being a senior executive or going on the lecture circuit. Often younger people find this "letting go" hard to understand and see it as

---

[84] "The Development of Personality," *The Development of Personality,* CW 17, par. 290.

a kind of accommodation to age. Instead, I would call it one of the rewards of age. The child of the future begins to know what is really essential and to trust these desires for intimacy and privacy.

Stage Seven is "Generativity vs. Stagnation." One develops an interest in establishing and guiding the next generation.

> Only he who in some way has taken care of things and people and has adapted himself to the triumphs and disappointments adherent to being, by necessity, the generator of things and ideas . . . may gradually grow the fruit of these seven stages.[85]

The fruit, according to Erikson, is Stage Eight, "Ego Integrity vs. Despair." If one has ego integrity, there is a sense of order and meaning, in both a worldly and spiritual sense, as well as a sense of one's own life cycle as something that had to be as it was. The past, including parents and life experiences from birth to the present, is accepted in a new way. Erikson calls this "accrued ego integration." Lack of this kind of integration shows itself as despair. Sometimes disgust hides one's despair and fear of death. But when the eighth stage is achieved, ego accrues order, meaning and trust in self and others. This, of course, is the ideal. It is seldom achieved, but it is a model worthy of consideration.

Other developmentalists have posited their own theories about age, adding their ideas to the foundations laid by pioneers like Erikson. Psychologist and anthropologist David Gutmann wrote in 1981 of "the growth potentials of aging" as a special form of creativity, an ability we all have to give form and reality to the essence of life. With age, he says, one gains a maturing ability to connect with one's own inner priorities and to mediate them to others. With a special ability to make nonmaterial traditions and myths come alive for the young, elders can give meaning to the lives of future generations. He reports that in tribal cultures the old people are the guardians of the mysteries and the laws. They are the storytellers who pass on the songs and sagas of age-old traditions, "the sacred or totemic aspect" of culture, giving context to the life of the tribe. "By making the sacred real, the

---

[85] *Childhood and Society,* p. 231.

aged make the secular ways palatable and dignified."[86]

"How does the matter stand with us?" asks Jung:

> Where is the wisdom of our old people? Where are their precious se-
> crets and their visions? For the most part our old people try to com-
> pete with the young. In the United States it is almost an ideal for a
> father to be the brother of his sons, and for the mother to be if pos-
> sible the younger sister of her daughter.[87]

Thus we neglect our task as bearers and mentors of creativity in ourselves and in others.

Roger Gould, psychiatrist and gerontologist, notes that though individuals never reach their full potential, they never stop pushing in
that direction. As long as we're moving along in life at a pretty
steady pace, we feel fairly good about life, subject of course to daily
fluctuations and periodic tragedies. But when the desire to grow
comes into conflict with the desire to remain the same at all costs, we
are at war with ourselves. Then it is impossible to be a guardian of
the mysteries or to achieve integrity. When an older person gets
stuck in one stage of development, there is no going forward until
the tasks of that stage have been achieved. Until then one is blocked,
feeling anxious or experiencing what Gould calls "baffling psychosomatic symptoms that warn us to remain within the constricted, safe
self, the self as others have known us."[88]

Jungians often speak to and about being stuck at various stages of
development. Many contemporary Jungians were originally educated
in developmental theory, and others, coming from a classical Jungian
background, have incorporated the work of early childhood developmentalists like Melanie Klein and D.W. Winnicott into their analytic practices. Klein, Winnicott and other object relations theorists
are rich sources not only for those who work therapeutically with
children but also for those who work with aging adults. Winnicott's

---

[86] "Psychoanalysis and Aging: A Developmental View," pp. 493-494.

[87] "The Stages of Life," *The Structure and Dynamics of the Psyche,* CW 8,
par. 788.

[88] "Transformational Tasks in Adulthood," p. 57.

"false self" can be just as evident in the life of a sixty-five year old as in a child. A person of fifty or sixty can be as much in need of celebratory mirroring as any narcissistic four year old, because such mirroring is a requisite for all growth and development.

When the trauma of life events, including the shock of coming to age, shatters one's old self-image and ego attitudes, the deeper psychological work of transition must be preceded by ego reinforcement and stabilization. Also, regression can occur at any age, often calling for therapy based on the theoretical models of early childhood development, object relations or self psychology.

Andrew Samuels sees Jungians as visualizing personal development in three ways: linear, spiral or circular. Linear developmental theory assumes that each stage requires a new adaptation of ego to society and to the world at large. Life events shape the personality as one moves along a more or less straight path from birth to death. Erikson's model is an example. A model derived from Jung is described by Samuels as the spiral paradigm, based on "a system with opportunity for new elements to enter."

- In the spiral the same elements interact with each other but at a different place with each repetition in the ascent. (For example, ego and self relate differently at different points.) The spiral also illustrates the way in which components of the psyche are operated upon by environmental demands.[89]

A paradigm of circular growth, believes Samuels, underlies James Hillman's school of archetypal psychology:

Behind Hillman's assertions to the contrary, there is a model of development in his work which is different from a linear model [stages, etc.] on the one hand and, on the other, from the notion of development as a spiral. . . . What is meant by circularity is that every element of the personality is seen as always present and as always having been so, and that development is construed as development of something into itself, into the nature that was always there.[90]

---

[89] *Jung and the Post-Jungians,* p. 115.
[90] Ibid., p. 141.

The two other important non-Jungian models are activity theory, attributed to Robert Havighurst and associates, and disengagement theory, developed from the research of Elaine Cumming and Lois Dean.[91]

Activity theory posits that people do not essentially change but seem to retain the attitudes and life styles of midlife as they age. This theory finds that people have the same needs in old age as at midlife, but physical and societal factors curtail the ability of individuals to satisfy those needs. The implication of this is that the majority of aging persons would choose to remain active if given the chance. If older people had the right outlets and encouragement, activity theory argues, they could remain high functioning in their later years. As a result, their life satisfaction would be high, meaning they would be happier and more productive. Such a theory resonates with the extraverted life style of American society.

Activity theory obviously affirms the high value our culture places on being busy and productive. Many centers established for the elderly in the United States plan activities based on this approach, helping older people keep physically and mentally involved through specially designed programs that reinforce established ego and persona strengths. These programs have been life-savers for many. Helpful as they are, however, they frequently overlook the importance of inner work or the necessity for psychological change as tasks of later life, assuming that it is best to stay active and unchanged as long as possible.

For some of those in transition, the theory of disengagement may be more applicable. This theory finds that the aging person experiences relief when societal demands lessen and the call for attention to body and psyche increases, thus giving permission to proceed with interior tasks. Disengagement theory assumes that it is easier and probably better for the aging person to go along with this desire for retreat and introversion. Then they can reach a new equilibrium in

---

[91] See Beatrice Neugarten, ed., *Middle Age and Aging;* Margaret Huyck and William Hoyer, *Adult Development and Aging;* and Elaine Cumming and William Henry, *Growing Old: The Process of Disengagement.*

which the demands of the outer world are no longer primary; rather the focus is on adapting to one's inner world and to the decline, fast or slow, of the physical body.

From a Jungian view it is possible to see the activity and disengagement theories as representative of extraverted and introverted ways of functioning. The extravert takes in information from events and data in the outer world, then processes that information and makes it his or her own. The introvert, on the other hand, processes information internally, assimilating it before placing it in an appropriate context in the world. Neither way is more valuable than the other. Both are necessary.

It is interesting to note that even disengagement theory reveals the extraverted orientation of our hyperactive culture in its use of the term "disengagement" to describe a more introverted stance. As James Hillman pointed out in a 1989 workshop in Boston:

> We live in an extraverted society where anything less than mania is considered depression. Fast food, fast cars, one-hour photo service and speed check-outs are only some of the testimony to our desire to make a hyperactive life style the norm.

For instance, when Ally, a young entry-level banker, complained to her boss that a sixty-hour week left her no time to recharge her batteries or have a life of her own, she was told, "This *is* your life. If you can't stand the pace, get out of the race." Such comments reflect a prevailing mentality that can be unbearable for the young, just as it is for those coming to age. As our bodies and minds slow down, it often becomes more and more difficult to cope with a hurried and harried world.

We who are students and practitioners of analytical psychology often find ourselves out of the mainstream of gerontological theory. Our support of introversion, descent and inner work is also frequently in direct opposition to the current emphasis on short-term interventions. The slow unfolding process of our work does not always fit well with theoretical models based on extraversion and quick change, for we recognize depression and regression as vital to change. Thus those who focus on their own individuation, which may demand introversion and withdrawal, may be at odds not only with themselves but with society's values as well. The dissolving that takes place as part of the transition to *metanoia* may be made even more difficult if one has internalized values that affirm activity and see disengagement as pathological.

As therapists we must resist the temptation to turn away from older patients, to send them for tranquilizers or other medical Band-Aids, or prod them into extraverted activity, just as we would like to turn away from our own aging, relying on rigorous regimens of exercise and diet in the futile belief that we can hold back the ravages of time. Affirming the importance of inner work, most Jungians, however unattractive they may find the term "disengagement," find the theory itself, with its emphasis on turning inward, well suited to their view of the psyche.

My own experience is that activity theory and disengagement theory represent a split that is characteristic of the struggle to reach the *metanoia* of age. Activity and disengagement, like extraversion and introversion, become polarized when one cannot see and feel their interplay in the psyche. There are usually parts of the personality that want to remain active in the world. There is also, quite spontaneously it would seem, a need for withdrawal. Like systole and diastole, contraction and expansion, activity and withdrawal form a natural rhythm when this instinct has not been overridden. However, the finely-tuned, well-developed ego of a physically active older person seldom takes kindly to the regression or transformation of the personality that withdrawal facilitates. Hence those who retreat may need support in creating the space and time necessary for a late-liminal descent.

During the late-life transition, many feel that while a part of their ego is still actively participating in the everyday world, the rest of their personality seems to sink into the unconscious. While this happens to all of us to some extent whenever we approach a major change, it often seems to be more pronounced in the croning years. Many report themselves functioning pretty well in the outer world even as their inner self is engaged in deeply introverted tasks far from the outer scene.

An older woman analysand saw this time of descent and severe regression as a ritual drowning in a cauldron, a huge pot much like that of the three Fates in Shakespeare's *Hamlet,* or those of the Greek goddess Hecate and the Celtic goddess Ceridwen. The cauldron is well known as a vessel of transformation in which life events and the future all get "cooked up." At a time of extreme distress in her work the woman wrote this poem:

Drowning
   I fall forgotten
   Into the depths
   Of Her cauldron

Life
   No matter now
   Boils down
   In the black blood
     Of Her brew

Who then
   tends the fire
   stirs the pot
     And Waits?

Amplifying her imagery, we remember the three Fates and also Hecate as keepers of the cauldron in which change is stirred up. The analytic relationship is sometimes dreamed of as a transformative vessel or cauldron, especially as the work begins to heat up and "cook." When this happens, there can be images of dissolving or disintegrating, of being chopped up or boiled. Images of blood and people dying are not uncommon. The old way *is* dying as the new begins to form. Who, then, tends the fire, stirs the pot, and waits? We might say that the analyst often performs these tasks. But many older analysands find that they themselves contain the attendant ego that stirs the pot and monitors the process, gathering their dreams and attending their complexes with meticulous care even as they are in the depths of the work.

Often as I sit with such a person I am reminded of Ceridwen, the crone-queen-goddess of Celtic mythology and her helpers who do these tasks. Less well known to most of us than Hecate or the Fates, Ceridwen's story nevertheless amplifies and informs in a powerfully authentic way the transformation of coming to age.

Like Hecate, Ceridwen is an archetypal representation of the power of the feminine over beginnings and endings and new beginnings again. As a shape changer, she knows how to live in liminal spaces. As goddess and keeper of the cauldron, she guides us in our journeys into the depths and oversees our changes. She is a wise woman, a magician. Like Maria Prophetissa, one of the earliest alchemists, she reads her books and cooks her brews in search of wisdom and enlightenment. Where Maria wanted to make gold out of dross in her own life, however, Ceridwen wants to find the gold of enlightenment for her son, passing on to him and to future generations all the wisdom of the ages.

We meet the story of Ceridwen's transformative cauldron in many versions throughout the Celtic world, the most famous of which is the story of an ordinary boy named Gwion Bach who is transformed into the famous bard Taliesin.[92]

Ceridwen and her husband, the king, have an only son who is so ugly that they name him Afaggdu, which in Welsh means "utter darkness." The mother is unable to affirm him just as he is, especially since she knows that he will never be able to fulfill her greatest desire to be accepted at the court of the High King. For a very long time she ponders on how to make him presentable. There is no way to change his appearance. Finally, however, she comes up with a scheme to give him all the wisdom in the world, making him the wisest of the wise with a mind so great none will be able to resist him. Collecting rare herbs and plants at special hours each day, she puts them into her cauldron and slowly brews up a magic potion that an ancient spell book promises will cook down into three drops con-

---

[92] See, for instance, Patrick Ford, trans. and ed., *The Mabinogi and Other Medieval Welsh Tales,* pp. 162 ff.

taining the very essence of wisdom. If Ceridwen does her work faithfully for a year and a day, the spell cannot fail. Since she cannot find, collect and brew up her herbs plus keep the fire going and the pot stirred all by herself, she hires an old blind man who happens by to help her. He stirs the pot while his young, dumbling, boy-guide feeds the fire with wood collected nearby. This leaves Ceridwen free to gather each herb under the special conditions and at the particular hours laid out in her ancient spell book.

Viewing Ceridwen as ego, we see the difficulties of trying to cope with the extreme activity of outer tasks while keeping the vessel of the inner work heated and cooking. Help is needed if we are to both gather and cook. But just as Ceridwen's helpers are blind and dumb, so we may find ourselves depending on contents of our own psyches that have no view of outer reality and no sense of the meaning of what is going on. In a man the figures of the blind man and the boy might represent elements of the shadow. In a woman they might represent the animus, unconscious and undeveloped components of her masculinity. Either way they are indicative of unconscious activity that serves to further ego goals.

In the story, the gathering, stirring and feeding of the fire go on for a year and a day. Finally the time comes when the magic drops will coagulate out of the brew and the ugly one will be redeemed. Ceridwen sits down under a tree to wait, having stationed her dark son beside the cauldron where she thinks he can't miss being touched by his new destiny. But just before the crucial moment she falls asleep! And instead of the ugly son, it is the dumbling boy Gwion Bach who gets the three precious drops, some say by trickery, others by happenstance.

When she awakens, Ceridwen is enraged. But Gwion, having all the wisdom in the world, had realized that she would try to destroy him, so before she regains full consciousness he runs away. She runs after him. Again and again he changes shape, trying to elude her. Each time this happens, she changes into an appropriate predator. The chase goes on until Gwion becomes a kernel of corn and Ceridwen a hen who swallows him. With the corn seed in her belly, she becomes pregnant. Now she waits again, this time to kill Gwion as soon as he is born. But when the baby comes she finds him so beautiful that she cannot harm him. Neither can she keep him, for he has robbed her first-born of his chance at the life she longed to give him—acceptance at court and a place of power in the world. Ceridwen takes Gwion to the sea and sets him adrift in a tiny coracle. Eventually he is rescued by a prince who names him Taliesin, "The Radiant Brow," because he shines with beauty and wisdom.

The bright, creative animus comes into being despite all Ceridwen's determination to imbue the negative animus with knowledge and power. Her falling asleep is similar to what happens to the extravert when introversion takes over. It is Ceridwen's fall into the opposite of her conscious extraverted stance, her unconscious introversion, that brings unexpected transformation rather than fulfillment of her desire for power and glory.

In our own lives, going into the unconscious may bring awareness quite different from our expectations. The new consciousness may even make us angry until we have begun to identify and assimilate what has come to us. Especially as we search for wisdom in age, we need to be aware of whether our desire is to be more powerful in the world or to give birth to new creativity without placing a personal claim on it.

While Afaggdu, the dark son, disappears from Ceridwen's story almost as soon as he enters it, we find him again in a later story where he is King Arthur's right-hand man in battle. He needs no armor because stiff hair protects his entire body. The impenetrable Afaggdu covered with bristles symbolizes that part of psyche we undervalue and see only as ugly, yet want desperately to transform. While it is often bitter when we cannot redeem the darkest parts of ourselves, we also must recognize that these ugly and undervalued traits can sometimes protect us in our struggles to be conscious.

Who is it, then, in those of us who are older, who waits with Ceridwen for the distillation of all our gathering? Who is it who knows that ego is there, cooking in the depths, even as another "observing ego" keeps the fire going and the pot stirred? Who is it who stays awake, even as another falls asleep at the auspicious moment, thus allowing the trickster to do his work in bringing about an unexpected pregnancy and new birth in the psyche?

Often at important moments in our individuation, the observer in the psyche is projected onto the analyst while the analysand struggles with depression. Yet it has been my experience that the ego of many older people can carry much of their own awareness during their most profound descents. That ego awareness stirs the pot and feeds the fire, watching, even as another facet of ego sinks into a deep oblivion that seems like death. Sometimes both analyst and analysand have the feeling of standing outside the work even as both are being cooked.

Without denying the importance of activity, it needs to be said over and over by those of us who work from a Jungian orientation that the experience of disengagement and introversion is vital to individuation. To anyone well along on the journey this is obvious enough. Yet we must keep repeating it if we are to balance the scales on which the extremes of extraverted activity carry the weight of societal values.

In 1953 Florida Scott-Maxwell wrote of aging:

> Sitting in a decent silence, enjoying the presence of the you that does not talk, and liking even better the absence of the one that does. One's mind open, in case there is any peace about; but turning away from the too personal, in search of the impersonal—we need a good deal of blankness for that.[93]

Irene Claremont de Castillejo wrote that libido, meaning life energy, changes direction when old age approaches. Outer activities lose their glamour and the inner world demands attention. This demand can be so strong that one who refuses the call may become ill. If individuals coming to age take time out to "ruminate and ponder and put forth new shoots in an unaccustomed inner world,"[94] they may find new creativity awaiting them.

---

[93] "We Are the Sum of Our Days."
[94] *Knowing Woman: A Feminine Psychology,* p. 158.

It is in the latter part of life that people need to turn attention inwards. They need to do so because if their garden is as it should be they can die content, feeling that they have fulfilled their task of becoming the person they were born to be.[95]

Only then can they live their final years to the fullest, with integrity, even as the life of the body diminishes.

M. Esther Harding wrote of the need for a new guide to help the aging make the move away from past work, activity and "keeping young." She pointed out that the psychoanalytic schools of Freud and Adler may help one to adapt to youthful tasks, but Jung's views are more suited to the problems of older people. Detachment from matters of the outer world, rather than being a loss, is "a necessary condition of bringing to birth a spiritual creation no less important than the creations belonging to the earlier periods of life."[96] When we are unable to detach enough to tend to our spiritual development, we may find ourselves in the place that Roger Gould speaks of, that stuck place where we are "blocked and at war with ourselves." When this happens, he tells us, growth becomes a conflict.

When blocked for too long we become negative, sour joy killers dwelling on our inadequacies, consumed with envy and blaming others because we can't admit the powerful split within us.[97]

Few of us seek the role of "negative, sour joy killers" as we age. Why is it then that we so often find ourselves in just such a position, feeling anxious, ill and ill-tempered as we remain stuck? Gould explains:

When about to move out of the stuck position, or ironically when in the midst of a large or accelerated move, we experience anxiety and often other baffling psychosomatic symptoms that warn us to remain within the constricted, safe self, the self as others have known us.[98]

---

[95] Ibid., p. 161.
[96] *The Way of All Women*, p. 245.
[97] "Transformational Tasks in Adulthood," p. 57.
[98] Ibid.

What happens to us when we get stuck, caught in a dark, regressive side of aging—when we are unable to move through our anxiety and pain to a new attitude? Often our bodies draw us into the dark side of its need for attention. We begin to worry obsessively about our health even when we are physically well. Life energy seems to flow out from our bodies in a way we can't control. When we are exhausted we're apt to become psychologically and physically constipated, wanting to retain all of our creative output including what the body needs to expel. At times we also feel that we can't take in anything more and yet we are hungry to fill up the emptiness of the psyche, experiencing such emptiness somatically as a need to eat or drink, feeling starved even as we stuff ourselves. On the other hand, if we feel overstuffed with information and the bombardment of psychic energy of an extraverted world we may shut down, withdraw, refusing both food and relationship. We may, at the same time, try to feed others so that they are fattened up to feed us.

Jacqueline Schectman describes the Hansel and Gretel witch, "a woman older than the hills,"[99] in this fashion:

> The old woman in this tale keeps the mean, devouring aspect of her self well hidden, and stays with her sweet persona at least long enough to lure the hungry children in.[100]

> This sweetly devouring one lies so deep in the collective psyche that we see her everywhere.[101]

This is the grandmother who lives on the energy of her children and grandchildren, leaving them to wonder why they are so depleted after each visit, especially when she feels so much better after spending time with them. It is also the older man who keeps himself too busy to realize how often he drains the energy of others to replenish his own supply, rather than taking the necessary time to rest and acknowledge his own depletion or to be refilled from within himself.

When the negative hag gets constellated, be it in men or in

---

[99] *The Stepmother in Fairy Tales*, p. 68.

[100] Ibid., p. 67.

[101] Ibid., p. 69.

women, we often see what Jane Wheelwright describes as "the self-assertive ones . . . [who keep] grinding on and on in the face of the exasperation of those around them," or the timid ones, "poor things [who] scuttle out of sight at the slightest challenge."[102] They are two sides of the same coin. Both are aspects of what we fear—that change may bring us death rather than life, sadness rather than joy, bitter dregs rather than clear well-aged wine.

Ann and Barry Ulanov write of the dark side of aging in terms of "the hapless hag":

> [She] sounds themes that reverberate through all of witchdom: the reversal of the flow of life-energies, the making of nothing where there was something, effecting absence where there was presence. Instead of feeding children, this witch eats them to feed herself. Instead of caring for others, she sucks their life's blood from them to augment her own. . . . She schemes, she plots, she lusts after power.[103]

In all of us there is resistance toward such an all-containing, devouring, life- and death-dealing crone—that wicked stepmother who is the dark side of the unconscious. While we long for a return to the symbiosis we experienced in the womb, we wisely dread the loss of ego such a return would entail. We are respectfully afraid of that old Mother because she annihilates. She sweetens or fattens our lives only to feed herself. Our denigration of the aged may be an attempt to cover our fears and stave off the devouring aspects of the unconscious itself. Our obsession with body can be a desire to avoid the inevitability of death.

Jung stressed that it is of great importance for those who are coming to age to get "acquainted" with death. Commenting on a dream a sixty-year old woman had two months before she died, he wrote:

> [In the dream] she had entered the hereafter. There was a class going on, and various deceased women friends of hers sat on the front bench. An atmosphere of general expectation prevailed. She looked around for a teacher or lecturer, but could find none. Then it became

---

[102] *For Women Growing Older,* p. 38.
[103] *The Witch and the Clown,* p. 77.

plain that she herself was the lecturer, for immediately after death people had to give accounts of the total experience of their lives. . . .

. . . [Thus] a categorical question is being put to her, and she is under an obligation to answer it. To this end she ought to have a myth about death, for reason shows her nothing but the dark pit into which she is descending. Myth, however, can conjure up other images for her, helpful and enriching pictures of life in the land of the dead. If she believes in them, or greets them with some measure of credence, she is being just as right or just as wrong as someone who does not believe in them. But while the woman who despairs marches toward nothingness, the one who has placed her faith in the archetype follows the tracks of life and lives right into her death. Both, to be sure, remain in uncertainty, but the one lives against her instincts, the other with them.[104]

Or as Edgar Herzog says in *Psyche and Death:* "Only the man who is prepared in his soul to pass through the Gate of Death becomes a living human being."[105]

Surely these statements are as true of our descents into the unconscious as they are of our relation to death. Often we're terrified of the little deaths that precede transformation, because they feel like the advent of physical death. As one older woman put it, "Every time I'm in for a major change I think I'm dying."

Fear like this is often constellated by a complex, a collection of old attitudes partially in the personal and partially in the collective unconscious, that obstructs the flow of energy between ego and Self. This may be an old parental complex full of outgrown judgments and rules. Or it may be a complex that pulls us deep into the body where we're apt to feel that the only safety is in staying stuck there. As Gould points out in the passage quoted earlier, we are split within ourselves, terrified to move out of our old complexes and back into the flow of life that will inevitably carry us toward the death of our former way of being.

Jane Wheelwright speaks about the change in the relation between

---

[104] *Memories, Dreams, Reflections,* p. 305 (pronouns changed in second paragraph).
[105] *Psyche and Death,* p. 209.

ego and Self that comes with aging. The ego, even as it becomes a separate and distinct complex, is more open to the archetype of the Self as we age.[106] This change in the relationship accords with the experience of being both in the descent and outside as an observing ego. Edward Edinger writes of this as two kinds of knowing:

> 1) the experience of being the knowing subject and 2) the experience of being the known object. One could say that we begin our psychic existence in the unconscious state of known object and only laboriously, with the growth of the ego, achieve the relatively tranquil status of knowing subject.
> . . . The process of becoming conscious requires both seeing and being seen, knowing and being known.[107]

Edinger sees the purpose of life as growth in consciousness, which means "knowing together with another." In religion that other is God. In Jung's terminology the other with whom we seek a knowing relationship is the Self.

An older person seeking such a relationship may feel both more intense involvement and more detachment. Ego is both stronger and humbler before the Self. There can be new self-perceptions as one reformulates ideas about life and death. Many voices seem to bear this out, telling us that while it is important to remain active, reformulating our ideas and attitudes in later life usually entails a descent in which energy is turned inward and unconscious complexes and outgrown attitudes are dismantled. Often aging entails a time of introversion and reassessment. This may involve an extended hermitage or simply withdrawal for an hour or two a day.

At the late-liminal stage of life, our bodies seem particularly to draw our attention inward. As we quiet ourselves and become more meditative, we become more aware of our breathing, our fatigue or strength, our aches and pains. If we ignore our aging bodies and the symptoms they produce, those very symptoms may force us to take notice. If we pay attention, a slow wonder often develops at how the

---

[106] "Old Age and Death," pp. 10ff.
[107] *The Creation of Consciousness,* pp. 52-53.

body works and what it contains.

Problems of heart, vascular system, respiratory tract, or bone, not uncommon in an aging population, may necessitate hospitalization. If we are conscious enough not to ignore the call of what Jung called our vocation, we may recognize that our bodies are signaling a transition, calling us to introversion, to transformation, and eventually to the great change of conscious attitude that is *metanoia*.

As we age we are invited to the Ceridwen's cauldron of our own bodies and souls, and while we may not, like Gwion Bach, find enlightenment, we will certainly experience changes that prepare us for the years ahead. Like Ceridwen, we may even find a surprising creativity gestating and coming to birth in us as we seek new ways to embody the opposites—the youngster of our childhood along with the crone, the bristly dark youth and his radiant sibling, the good and evil of our long lives—in short, all that we have accepted and all that we have rejected coming together to form what we are yet to be.

5

The Aging Body

Around age fifty-five or sixty, the body of even the healthiest person may experience strange symptoms. A niggling stiffness in joints, unpleasant after-effects from certain foods, slower recovery from minor illnesses, all gently call for attention. Our energy level fluctuates. One minute we feel ready to lick our weight in wildcats, the next we can only sink exhausted into a chair.

Ignoring these signs and pushing on in our usual fashion may lead to illness, for the body is demanding conscious attention, sending messages that cannot be ignored. Eventually the intensity of symptoms forces us to stop and take notice. It's time to slow down and reassess our life. We may even have to undergo hospitalization, "a lying-in" period, to await the birth of a new way of being.

Gerontologists have long agreed on the importance of a life review.[108] To date, however, the connection between integrity and work with the physical and imaginal body has had minimal attention. Jungian analysts like Joan Chodorow, Anita Greene, Arnold Mindell and Marion Woodman have discovered in their work with the body that memories are stored in our organs, our bones, our muscles and our cells as well as in our brains. Greene writes:

> My long experience with body work has demonstrated to me how certain images and memories, both positive and negative, are so imprisoned in body tissue that they may never appear in the analytical work until released through touch.[109]

Body-centered therapies like massage, breath work, therapeutic touch, acupuncture and others too numerous to name all support Greene's observation. Nevertheless, this information is frequently

---

108 See, for instance, Robert Butler, *Why Survive?: Being Old in America.*
109 "Giving the Body Its Due," p. 16.

greeted with skepticism and anxiety by experienced clinicians who see the dangers such work introduces into transference-counter-transference dynamics. Many find it hard to believe there can be such a thing as safe touch.

Most of us are deprived when it comes to our own physicality. We are still learning very slowly how to honor the messages our bodies deliver. The very thought that our hips or knees might hold long-forgotten memories that could be released by touch causes shudders of anxiety.

For hundreds of years we in the West have been taught to deny the flesh. "Mind over matter" is a time-honored maxim. True body wisdom has been carefully ignored or denied along with the flesh itself. Every magazine gives us methods of ridding ourselves of undesirable pounds. The general result is that the body and its functions have been relegated to the shadow side of life, regarded as dark and possibly even evil. As Jung points out:

> The body is a most doubtful friend because it produces things we do not like; there are too many things about the body which cannot be mentioned. The body is very often the personification of this shadow of the ego. Sometimes it forms the skeleton in the cupboard, and everybody naturally wants to get rid of such a thing.[110]

We need our animal selves, our bone, muscle and instinct-laden physicality to survive on this planet. One wonders why we as a culture have become so anti-body, as if our very flesh were a disease against which we must wage war. Writes Jung:

> If we are still caught by the old idea of an antithesis between mind and matter, the present state of affairs means an unbearable contradiction . . . . But if we can reconcile ourselves to the mysterious truth that the spirit is the living body seen from within, and the body the outer manifestation of the living spirit—the two being really one— then we can understand why the striving to transcend the present level of consciousness through acceptance of the unconscious must give its due to the body.[111]

---

[110] "The Tavistock Lectures," *The Symbolic Life,* CW 18, par. 40.
[111] *Modern Man in Search of a Soul,* p. 253.

One might guess that as the old more matriarchal forms of religion were replaced, the body was also denigrated. My fantasy is that in the beginning humankind worshipped the earth and the elements, telling stories, feeling awe, seeing all beings as One. There was no separation of body, mind or spirit, and no individuals. Everything was One, and eventually this One was imaged as a Mother who contained all being within her vast body. Life and death were birthed out of the caves that were her womb. Her burgeoning breasts gave food. Her enormous legs and buttocks and torso made up the mountains and hills of an earthly landscape. Even the sky was her belly. Every cell of her gigantic body was alive with Her messages, Her gifts.

But in humankind's development, a time came when She began to be perceived as a separate being, perhaps even periodically absenting Herself, as a mother inevitably must at times leave her child. Images and statues of Her began to proliferate as "transitional objects" to comfort the people when the presence of the Great Mother was no longer felt in the world and in their bones. Just as this abandonment experience is terrifying for a baby intimately bonded with its actual mother, the perception of the Great Mother's absence created upheaval for humankind. Just as a baby experiences absence as death, so humankind went through a "Goddess is dead" phase. Slowly, during this time when the Great Mother was felt to be absent, humans began to believe that they, the world and the Mother were not always One. Sometimes they and the Mother were two. Sometimes they and other objects were two.

As this happened, an unconscious need to banish or kill off the original oneness began to arise so that "twoness" could come into being. The Great Mother began to be perceived as a dark, suffocating, all-absorbing other: a monster. The need for a hero to do battle and to defeat her gave rise to myths of killing the dragon or serpent. For centuries many terrible purges attempted to cleanse the collective psyche of ancient goddess worship that honored the female body as the matrix in which there were no divisions. Fear of the unconscious was projected onto that body in such forms as siren, enchantress, witch, hag and devouring mother.

When mind and spirit were split from body it was in the hope that the heroic mind-spirit would triumph over matter. New religions that we now call patriarchal, like those of the Judeo-Christian tradition, arose to lead humankind away from its unconscious identification with the Mother. Just as the father leads the child out of early, unconscious bonding with the maternal, "as a reminder of the world outside,"[112] so Western humanity went through a developmental stage that brought it, symbolically, out of the Garden of Eden—out of the matrix of the collective unconscious—into a new level of awareness in which spirit and body were poles apart. Sin was perceived not so much as a greediness for consciousness as a seduction through sexuality. If it hadn't been for Physis, Matter, Mother or Eve, we might all be floating around as happily disembodied spirits without having to carry the burden of flesh and earthly desires!

Because the monster of flesh had to be "mortified," women had to be kept in their place, especially powerful old crones, for they were the ancient tribal matriarchs who carried the archetypal projections of the Wise Old Great Mother; they knew the mysteries of how life in the body came and went, and could give life and take it away.[113]

In Greece the archetypal image of this crone figure was called Hecate, Queen of the Dead, Great Midwife of Birth, Death and Transformation. Other goddesses carried the same projection. Even Hera, Queen of Heaven in the Greek pantheon, was identified as one who brought death. In Germany this figure was called Hel or Angurboda, whose dogs carried off the souls of the dead much as Anubis did in Egypt. Throughout the world she was feared and fought but never vanquished, always rising again from the unconscious. She could not be destroyed, only distorted into dangerous imagery. But the women who were faithful to Her could be methodically purged. This persecution culminated in the witch hunts of the Middle Ages and still goes on today in subtler form—the subjugation of natural forces, rape of the land and contamination of seas.

---

[112] Andrew Samuels, ed., *The Father,* p. 28.
[113] See Walker, *The Crone,* pp. 43ff.

Nevertheless, there is a resurgence of interest today not only in Her Body, the World and the treasures she contains, but in the human body as well. Many people have become deeply interested in what their bodies hold, and in finding ways to heal the split between the Mother Goddess who contains the embodied richness of all nature and the Father God who leads us toward a more spiritual consciousness of that nature. Thus more and more analysands are combining some kind of body work with analysis, and analysts have begun to recognize how vital touch, sometimes physical, sometimes imaginal, can be to our well-being. As Hyemeyohsts Storm writes:

> To touch and to feel is to Experience. Many people live out their entire lives without ever really Touching or being Touched by anything. These people live within a world of mind and imagination that may move them sometimes to joy, tears, happiness or sorrow. But these people never really Touch. They do not live and become one with life.
>
> . . . The six grandfathers taught me that each man, woman and child at one time was a Living Power that existed somewhere in time and space. These Powers were without form, but they were aware. They were alive.
>
> . . . These living Medicine Wheels were capable of nearly anything. They were beautiful and perfect in all ways except one. They had no understanding of limitation, no experience of substance. . . . They were placed upon this earth that they might Learn the things of the Heart through Touching.[114]

Physical touch is a concretization of the meeting of soul and spirit. Soul and spirit are given form in this way. There is, as most therapists recognize, a moment when psychologically the two come together. In the analytic container this touching of soul is abused if acted out sexually. It is equally abused if, through fear, the therapist mishandles it. The ability to allow eros to suffuse the analytic relationship without moving it onto a personal level requires respect for appropriate boundaries on the analyst's part and trust on the part of the analysand. When handled with the integrity of true *agape* love,

---

[114] *Seven Arrows,* p. 7.

nonphysical contact can often be far more profound than actual touch, more healing than the greatest insight. To sit with eros fully present, held but not acted out, may only happen for a moment at a time, but it leaves a lasting understanding for both analytic partners of what it means when the heart is truly touched.

For those trained in body work, who understand the boundaries, physical touch may properly be part of an analytic session.[115] The rest of us may instead work with body imagery and symbolism, which can immensely enrich any therapeutic hour. With an older analysand, this work becomes particularly rewarding as the body begins to trust enough to release its messages. Unfortunately many of the body messages we receive in our daily lives and practices are misunderstood. Touch is one of those most frequently misinterpreted. Many of us have been taught to interpret intimate touch only as sexual. We've forgotten that imaginal touch can often be just as powerful as flesh meeting flesh. Today we know the god Eros mostly in his sexual form, yet we honor him in relationship as the flow of libido that enlivens our deep connections with others.

It is fascinating to study the messages of the body in the liminal space of the therapeutic imagination, where registering and imaging one's own and another's body responses become as natural as monitoring thoughts and dreams. This is not a new practice thought up by analysts. It is an age-old technique used by shamen through the centuries. In Jamaica Mother Syckie prays and meditates with those who come to her for help, opening herself until she begins to feel what her patient is feeling. When this happens, she naturally begins to experience whatever strong emotions or sensations are held within the interactive field, feeling them in her own body and psyche. If there is a problem with her patient's eyes or ears, for example, she feels it in her own vision or hearing. Sometimes such somatic transference can be very painful and debilitating. Mother Syckie acknowledges that it is often extremely difficult to distinguish between what belongs to

---

[115] See, for instance, Deldon Anne McNeely, *Touching: Body Therapy and Depth Psychology.*

the patient and what to herself, but she knows this work of sorting out is something healers must do, a challenge we must meet if we are to help those who come to us.

When we allow ourselves to approach the analytic work in this way, it becomes especially grounded and enriched. Transference and countertransference begin to be expressed in a silent somatic language. Rather than physically acting out the powerful energies of relationship, we discover the intense reward of holding them in our own bodies and imagination. This requires that the analyst monitor his or her own body responses before, during and after each session. Often the analyst must hold the images as they grow more and more intense, choosing with utmost care the moments in which the sharing of such images might be helpful and appropriate.

Rachel, a woman moving toward the late-liminal years, is a high functioning professional with a powerful animus. As a positive transference began to build in our analytic work together, she asked to be hugged at the end of each session. When this seemed like acting out and I stopped it, she felt deprived and unloved. As an echo of early childhood abandonment that could cause intense pain, this reenactment plunged her into an old defense of shutting off affect, working only from her intellect, her competent self. We were stuck.

For weeks the resistance of her animus wordiness dominated our sessions. I could feel her determination to wear me down. Often it was as if we were both lifted about two feet off our chairs or buzzing about the room like caged birds. I felt the full measure of her desperate need to be held and contained. Week after week I struggled with my own responses, the desire to give in, to make everything okay again, to be a nurturing mother who would fulfill all her needs.

Finally she had this dream:

> In a warm room a therapist friend and I are taking off layer after layer of warm winter clothing until we are naked, flesh to flesh, face to face, talking in the most intimate fashion. As long as we stay connected in this way, I feel that I can tell her anything and she will understand. In the dream this feels perfectly natural, but as soon as I wake up I feel that this will be a difficult dream to present.

What do we do with this dream? At first glance it seems like an overt plea for the very thing I am refusing. I have a strong desire to avoid working with it. Like the hug, it is too hot to handle. I'm tempted simply to add it to her file without comment. Yet her psyche is giving me a metaphoric image of her desperate need for intimacy. She wants us to be naked, nothing hidden. She wants to feel her own embodiment by getting close to mine. She also seeks the early fusion of the child nestled against the breast, feeling the mother's breath and heartbeat as if they were her own, experiencing her own body by knowing that of the mother.

If we knew no imaginal metaphor for the pull and the emotion Rachel feels, we might both see her longing as "nothing but" sexual. Eros was powerful in our relationship, as it often is when the work pulls us toward true touching. Like the erotic embracing figures that grace the temples of India, the first stage of *coniunctio* is the acting out sexually of a deep psychic longing for union. Knowing this, the wise elders of that culture put sexual activity right where it belonged, on the outer side of the mysteries, the very earliest and most enticing step toward enlightenment.

Instead of denying or running away from the pull between us, Rachel and I begin to explore the meaning of the dream with body imagination. We talk about the vessel that contains our coming together, and how we can be faithful to the integrity of that container and to the union struggling to take shape imaginally within it.

I begin to check out my own body before each session, asking myself: Where do I feel tension? Where do I feel a twinge or an ache, numbness or a need to shift position? Throughout the session I try to be aware of my responses. When Rachel is in an animus mode, what do I feel in my body? When she connects with her own affect, is my body carrying it too? I discover that when we really connect, I begin to feel not only a sexual response but also extreme anxiety. This belongs to me. It also belongs to her, for as soon as we "touch," in the imaginal sense of exchanging energy in an intimate psychological relationship, she feels intensely anxious as well. When asked for images, she imagines falling into the dark places in her body as falling down a chute into a coal bin, a childhood fear/dream/fantasy. The pain and fear of suffocating under all that coal brings up affect that really seems to have been at the bottom of a deep shaft for most of her life—her feminine energy buried in fossilized form.

Gradually we move into a new phase of analysis, but still with great attention to our bodies and their responses, paying particular attention to the transference and countertransference.

Obviously such work takes a different form in each case. Working with the body in this fashion almost always carries both analyst and analysand into very deep areas indeed. For one analysand it was into the depths of a cave. For another it was down many ladders to an opening that led to the sea. For a third it was into the earth to an opening among the roots of the World Tree. In each case there was a descent that led to a profound experience of embodiment and reconnection with the earth and childhood imaginations. As one woman exclaimed, "As a child I was always told I was too imaginative, so I buried it. Now I feel as if I've come across a treasure."

In one case, with a cancer patient who needed distance in the early stages of the work, sandplay was used to facilitate the imagination of body. Slowly the sand tray contents could be related to what was going on in her body and the physical and emotional pain she felt. Indeed, pain is one of the body's most powerful messages, yet we spend countless hours and vast sums of money in efforts to be rid of it. One of the most important tasks for older people is to allow their bone, sinew and cells the freedom to express that pain as well as the anger and grief that the body stores. For the imaginally deprived, this is long slow work, not a quick fix. Alfred Ziegler writes:

> When [disease] is treated unquestioningly through the removal of symptoms, experience shows that we can count on considerably more relapses and complications than when respect is given to the disease. . . . the disease has a point to make![116]

Body symptoms often do need to be alleviated through medical treatment. But too often we either don't know or forget that they can

---

[116] *Archetypal Medicine,* p. 70.

also be symbolic messages if not psychosomatic: we repress them until they become pathological enough to demand notice. If we listen to our aging body and its pain, respectfully opening ourselves to symptoms, we may hear something astonishing calling us to descend into our physical being, to take time out to recuperate and listen to the Self. The inner wisdom that speaks through our bodies may be trying to point out new tasks that await us.

How might we facilitate this communication?

Keeping track of dreams is one method. Amplifying dream images that appear to come from, or be about, the body and noticing any affect evoked opens communication in ways sometimes quite unexpected. It's as if we free up energy in the unconscious by our willingness to articulate ideas and imagery that reflect the Self. Another way is to be aware of body responses and gestures during a therapy session. Body language is especially important, for often words give one message while the body gives another, sometimes quite unconsciously. It would seem that unconscious body communication is a field we could all explore to advantage. The authors of a book about this subject write:

> For those who can see and understand, the body speaks clearly, revealing character and a person's way of being in the world. It reveals past trauma and present personality, feelings expressed and feelings unexpressed.[117]

> On the deepest level, change *always* involves the body. A new attitude means new perceptions, new feelings, and new muscular patterns. Psychological and physiological change go hand in hand. Since our deepest traumas are imbedded in our guts and muscles, to free ourselves we must free our bodies.[118]

Jung's technique of active imagination helps to free the body to communicate about the growth and transformation underway.[119] The

---

[117] Ron Kurtz and Hector Prestera, *The Body Reveals: What Your Body Says About You,* preface.

[118] Ibid., p. 145.

[119] See "The Transcendent Function," *The Structure and Dynamics of the Psyche,* CW 8, pars. 166-175, and Barbara Hannah, *Encounters with the*

use of this technique can have profound effects for an aging patient, especially as his or her ability to image body responses begins to develop.[120] Usually this requires a letting go and allowing energy to flow into the unconscious, thereby activating the transcendent function. For many it is an experience of opening to unconscious areas of one's own physical being and to old matter held in our cells, so what is stored can be released physically and imaginally from the flesh-and-bone memory bank.

Imaginally reworking what the body has stored of trauma and triumph in a long series of life events is a most important step toward achieving integrity.

Soul: Active Imagination as Developed by C.G. Jung.
[120] A striking example of this process appears in Albert Kreinheder, *Body and Soul: The Other Side of Illness,* which describes the author's dialogues with his body during years of suffering from cancer and arthritis.

6

Active Imagination: The Dragon Body

Meg, an older woman who was a dancer and a singer, came to her session one day with acute bronchitis. She had a tight chest and a deep, racking cough. Her dreams seemed to have dried up. She felt depleted and out of sorts, both inside and out, cut off from her body and psyche. "I would have stayed home," she reported, "but I felt too bereft."

Having had several years of analysis with emphasis on dream work and active imagination, Meg decided to try to imagine herself within her symptom. Going imaginally into her upper chest and throat, she soon found herself on a bridge that arched over a raging fire in the depths of her lungs. She could feel the intense heat of the flames that seemed to rage out of control, barely contained within the space of her lungs and bronchi.

At the time Meg presented this image I was also seeing Claire, the patient mentioned in chapter two, who was suffering extremely distressing and debilitating symptoms in the upper chest because of chronic bronchial asthma. I immediately felt a connection between her area of discomfort and Meg's. In the course of several meetings, as Meg held her image and waited to see what happened, several of my younger patients, one after another, began to identify pain, depression and loneliness as "a dark hole in the upper chest."

In the Eastern symbolic system of Kundalini,[121] the energy center of the chest is the heart center, the place where one begins to experience ego in relationship. The throat chakra, a bit above, is the area of expression, of saying what needs to be said, especially about one's relationship with the Self. It is also the place of connection and relatedness between head and body.

---

[121] See, for instance, Gopi Krishna, *Kundalini: The Revolutionary Energy in Man.*

As sometimes happens when analyst and analysand imaginally occupy the therapeutic vessel together, within a short time I too began to develop a bronchial cough that was severe enough to interrupt sessions and cause distress to me and my patients. The synchronicity of all of these events brought Meg's image to my mind over and over again. I found myself struggling with a strong, somatized countertransference that seemed to put me on that very bridge, looking down into the same kind of fire in my own lungs. What message was psyche trying so hard to give us? What response could we give?

Many centuries ago, Tantric yogins in the East "imagined" the body as a somatic and psychic being. They anthropomorphized what Western psychologists might call the archetype underlying body/soul consciousness as a sleeping goddess, the Devi Kundalini. They saw her energy form as a coiled serpent asleep in the depths of the perineum, at the base of the spinal column. In extraordinarily artistic imagery, these Eastern yogins, over centuries of meditation and practice, began to codify their experiences of the awakening and rising of this serpentine energy within themselves. In the first of a series of lectures on Kundalini yoga that he gave with Jung in the early thirties, J.W. Hauer speaks of the variety of their descriptions as

> the grasping of certain radical processes of man's becoming, so strange, so deep, so absolutely inexpressible, that the help of the symbol was needed as a form to explain them, that they might be handed down to the coming generations. First the inner reality is grasped, then the symbol is used to crystallize this in the imagination, and [only] then comes the real practice of meditating the six chakras.[122]

Hauer describes chakras as an ancient concept of "mystic circles" in the human body and soul.[123] These circles, often called spheres, are specific centers located in *the body* where yogins have experienced a transformation of energy. I put *the body* in italics because they both are and are not of the physical body. They are usually ex-

---

[122] *Kundalini: Notes on the Seminar Given with Prof. J.W. Hauer*, pp. 13-14.
[123] Ibid., p. 57.

perienced as within one's physical body, sometimes as a slow warming but other times as a rush of energy that can feel quite painful. Anyone who has experienced active imagination happening inside the psyche as well as synchronistically in the outer world will understand that these events are not confined to the human physical body or to the personal psyche.

When the goddess Kundalini "awakens," she rises through the mystic imaginal spheres called chakras, fructifying and bringing life to each area of body and soul represented. Some have called the Devi Kundalini "energy." She is usually depicted in her serpent form, rising through one of three intertwined channels (that look remarkably like a Western medical caduceus). Hauer speaks of the nascent Kundalini as "waiting in the whole region of woman power." As wisdom she is "always waiting but asleep, not sleeping as dead matter, but sleeping as that humming being that makes a thrill throughout the universe."[124] The chakras through which she rises are often drawn as mandalas, each with its own identifying color, animal, sound, description and name.

The first sphere is called the *muladhara* chakra. This is the base chakra. Here the goddess energy lies sleeping in the roots at the base of the spinal tree, where everything is undifferentiated and unconscious, without form. This can be seen as the archetypal foundation, imprinted but inert. Jung tells us that the character of *muladhara* "is complete unconsciousness, complete mystical identity with the object, no differentiation whatsoever."[125]

The second center through which energy rises is *svadhisthana,* the water chakra. Jung's description of the collective unconscious seems to coincide with this sphere. It is the ocean that contains all life, the place where the fish of undeveloped contents swim in the depths. It is the deeps of mystery where one can be drowned, or reborn, or both. It is perceived to be located in the genital region. Between this chakra and the next seems to be a place where the moon rises, giving

---

124 Ibid., p. 98.
125 *The Visions Seminars,* p. 452.

a lunar awareness that is intuitive, but not yet fully conscious.

Manipura, in the region of the solar plexus, is the third chakra. This is the fire center, the place where things rising toward consciousness begin to cook. Jung calls it the kitchen, and also "where the sun rises."[126] We might say that it is where the personal unconscious has its beginning. Between *manipura* and the next chakra is what M. Esther Harding described as "a little by-path that leads to an altar where old ego goals must be sacrificed if one is to go on."[127]

Anahata, the fourth mystic sphere, is the place where the pulse of life is felt and the flame of consciousness begins to burn as an individual light spark. This is the area in which one begins to claim and differentiate one's own emotions. "Yes, I am in a bad mood." "Yes, I got caught in a complex." This is the heart chakra. Jung calls it "the center where psychical things begin, the recognition of values and ideas."[128] In *manipura* we are identical with the physical. There is little differentiation between self and other. In *anahata* we begin to comprehend the psychological and to realize that we are not the same as the other even though we are similar. We are able to imagine.

The fifth chakra, *visuddha,* is in the area of the upper chest and larynx. Arnold Mindell describes this center.

> The *Visuddha* is located in the throat plexus. This is the "purification" center, experienced as ether, air, wind and a door that swings back and forth without cause. Typical problems associated by many authors with this area are depression and speech trouble. The voice is easily disturbed by the persona or social mask since the natural sounds of the voice do not often conform to the effect one wants to create.[129]

To paraphrase Jung, when we begin to experience others as mirrors in which we see our projections, we are approaching *visuddha.* When we see that it is our subjective experience that gives us our

---

[126] Ibid., p. 163.

[127] Unpublished tape of a lecture on Kundalini yoga (by permission of Alma Paulsen-Hoyer).

[128] *Kundalini,* p. 181.

[129] *Dreambody: The Body's Role in Revealing the Self,* pp. 42-43.

view of others, and learn that others are often hooks on which we hang our own garments, we are on the way to *visuddha*. If we think that the world is substantial, without realizing that a table or chair or door is molecules in motion, we are still in *manipura* or *anahata*. In *visuddha* we are like the gazelle, "an animal of earth, but almost liberated from the power of gravity."[130]

The last two chakras—*ajna*, symbolizing the third eye, and *sahasrara*, the thousand-petal lotus at the top of the head, signifying enlightenment—are, Jung believed, quite beyond the comprehension of most Westerners.[131]

After Meg and I discussed the Kundalini we worked on the lung-fire image with active imagination. She continued to do this at home, and after taking a course of antibiotics began to recover. Identifying the fire in her respiratory system as anger, Meg began to express some things that needed to be said, even fought over, in her family, her job and her work with me. For her, the symptoms had fulfilled their purpose and she could move on to other issues. I, on the other hand, was left with both the symptoms and the image. For weeks I kept finding myself standing on a bridge within my own imaginal body, over the depths of my lungs, where red hot fires raged. It seemed as though hell itself had broken loose in my chest. My cough worsened, bringing on fever and fatigue, forcing me to rest.

Then one morning in meditation a thunderbolt struck: I realized I was in the body of an ancient dragon! The fire was dragon breath. My dream ego was on a bridge over an inferno within the lungs of a dragon. Something archaic, fantastic and powerful was raging within me, and even as I contained it, it also contained me. What was the treasure it guarded in my chest and throat?

As I pondered this, the memory of a conversation with a friend some years before came back, a woman who never had much formal schooling but who was deeply connected to life. One day as we sat over coffee she said to me:

---

130 *Kundalini*, pp. 190-191.
131 Ibid., p. 197.

"This morning I was thinking when I woke up, Why, I didn't even have to start my heart today! It just goes all by itself. It seems like a miracle, doesn't it? I don't have to push a button to get my lungs to breathe. I don't have to say, 'Okay, stomach, start digesting that food.' I don't even have to think about it. It all just happens!"

Was the dragon in which I found myself part of what "just happens"? If I was in that dragon, wasn't I somehow maintained by what thanatologists describe as "the snake awareness" at the base of the brain that can keep the body functioning long after the conscious personality is considered dead? Back in the seventies an ongoing debate was triggered by the case of a young girl in a coma who was apparently brain dead while being kept alive through life support systems. Was life the same as consciousness? Was activity in the brain stem, the "snake consciousness," a sign that the patient was still "alive"? What was this maintaining force within my body that kept me alive and functioning?

I began to explore imaginally what it would be like to have a dragon as the control center of my physical embodiment, a being both primitive and fantastic that at that moment appeared to be breathing fire, pulling my attention to the upper chest with powerful symptomatology.

Jung wrote of the dragon's symbolic importance:

> The serpent as well as the dragon and other reptiles usually symbolize those parts of the human psyche which are still connected with the animal side of man. The animal still lives in him: it is the old saurian that is really the dragon, and therefore the dragon is a very proper symbol. These parts of the psyche are most intimately connected with the life of the body and cannot be missed if body and consciousness are to work together soundly.[132]

The image of my body as dragon began to take on its own power. Feeling anxious, I tried to fix myself in the scene as ego, only to discover, as with the woman who wrote the poem of the cauldron, that there seemed to be more than one ego. Even as my dream ego was

---

[132] *Letters,* vol. 1, p. 485.

blown about, another part of me stood entirely apart, observing the action, struggling to understand but not interfere.

In trying to locate this observer, I realized to my utter astonishment that *it was not confined to my body,* yet somehow tended the process and awaited the outcome. Intellectually I had known of this concept for some time, but now it was experienced in a way that seemed to turn my inner world totally around. I knew the observer to be me, just as the tiny figure on the bridge was me. Both could be identified as ego, and it seemed that the transformation of one would also be the transformation of the other. For the first time I began to have a glimmer of what the term "subtle body" could mean in terms of aging and death.

Nathan Schwartz-Salant understands the subtle body to be both physical and spiritual:

> The question is not whether or not the subtle body exists, but whether or not its existence can be perceived. For when we deal with the subtle body, we are concerned not with ordinary perceptions but with imaginal ones.[133]

> [It] can manifest itself psychically in terms of dream, fantasy, and body images . . . and can manifest physically in terms of body structure and armoring.[134]

Schwartz-Salant reads Jung as saying that

> the shadow represents part of the psychological or psychic unconscious, while the subtle body represents the somatic unconscious, that is, *the unconscious that is experienced as we descend into the body.*[135]

What, then, in my active imagination, was the dragon into which I was imaginally descending? Ego was certainly in a physical body as well as outside as observer. Yet the "I" in the dragon seemed to be within a being that could keep my body going without ego control. At one level I felt I *knew* the "old saurian" that Jung describes, just

---

[133] *The Borderline Personality,* p. 133.
[134] Ibid., p. 135.
[135] Ibid., p. 137 (emphasis added).

as I *knew* my own body. At another level I was experiencing that gigantic, fantastic creature as if for the first time, and I hadn't the least idea what to do next.

For many years I have collected material amplifying the symbol of serpent and dragon. Only recently have I begun to realize the full extent to which this search has led me into the body, both in my own work and in work with older people. Like Lucifer, the fallen angel, the serpent (once a symbol for the *Nous,* the creative light and life-giving force) has come down to us in the Judeo-Christian tradition as dark, negative and cast out, condemned by God to crawl on its belly and be reviled by men. In the same manner, the dragon has been viewed through the patriarchal ages as evil personified. Legends of dragon slayings are familiar to us all, like the tale of St. Patrick driving the snakes out of Ireland. Dragons and serpents must be driven away, subdued or preferably slain. Yet as Jung wrote:

> It remains a question whether the dragon is to be considered as wholly evil. This question, however, is a most intricate one. . . . A certain amount—or better an uncertain amount—of darkness has to be allowed, because it is vitally necessary if the body or the mind is to live at all. Many neuroses come from the fact that too good a victory has been won over the body and its dark powers.[136]

One way of seeing the dragon is as embodiment, both physical and subtle. Looked at from this viewpoint, the centuries of attempting to kill the dragon take on an even greater mystery. This was the heroic task for mankind, reflected in legends throughout the West, from Perseus slaying the snake-haired Medusa to St. George spearing the dragons of Europe and the British isles.

Body must be "slain" in the service of mind and spirit. Flesh must be denied. Only in leaving the body could the soul be truly free. At the present time, in spite of so much value being given to the body and its maintenance, our ambivalence toward embodiment can be seen in the popular desire for "out-of-body" experiences and "astral travel." Meanwhile, a different consciousness is struggling to be

---

[136] *Letters,* vol. 1, p. 485.

born, a new yet ancient way of relating to the dragon/serpent of our somatic being.

In 1945 Ananda Coomaraswamy wrote an article in which he described a worldwide variety of legends that deal not with the slaying of the dragon but with an alternative, the *fier baiser,* or courageous kiss.[137] Rather than destroying the dragon/serpent, he suggests that the truly courageous hero must embrace the odious monster. Only when ego can accept the overtures of the Self in its most primitive, feared and loathsome form, without itself being destroyed or swallowed up, can ego truly be king. When one willingly embraces the "loathly worm" or "deadly dragon lady," she will respond by transforming herself into a great beauty, renewing both herself and the land.[138] This seems to be a way guided by an eros that serves the feminine rather than seeking, in fear, to destroy it. It takes a conscious connection with that eros to accept an approach so diametrically opposed to the instinctual urge to destroy or deny a loathsome symptom or body image.

In one fairy tale and legend after another the hero flees when asked to kiss the loathly maiden or the serpent queen. Each night she begs for his embrace. Each time he refuses, her form becomes more terrifying, she grows more heads, more scales, more girth. Finally the youngest brother is courageous enough to kiss or embrace her, or take her into his bed, whereupon she is transformed into a most beautiful woman who then bestows upon him dominion over a vast kingdom. This tale is told throughout the world. Only the one willing to embrace what is dark, archaic and terrifying can become a wise ruler, servant to the Queen of Nature.

Just as an heroic ego releases the princess from her ugliness through an eros strong enough to overcome fear and revulsion, it seems that we are asked to facilitate the transformation of the dragon of matter by our willingness to embrace even the ugliest and most unacceptable form in which it comes to us, be it Alzheimer's, cancer

---

[137] "On the Loathly Bride," pp. 395ff.
[138] See also Schectman, *The Stepmother in Fairy Tales,* pp. 18-19.

or any of the other plagues that threaten us as we age. Like the older brothers in fairy tales, we may run away, refusing our task. Hopefully, however, we can eventually return, like the youngest (typically a naive dumbling), and agree to embrace what is most loathsome to us. What would it mean for us to experience our bodies as dragons, filled with archaic power and untapped wisdom, keepers of treasure, in relationship with, yet uncontrolled by, the conscious ego? Faced with such a mighty force we too might recoil and flee.

Flight has always been a preferred defense. Colluding with symptoms so that the disease is left to act out the inner task is another. To turn the dragon into a toy, harmless in its cartoon sweetness, seems to mirror such an approach. "Oh, it's really not so bad. Nothing to be frightened about, nothing I can't easily ignore." But the dragon is powerful. We need to be aware that it can kill. When the call for transformation is ignored, especially later in life, the dragon can precipitate transformation in a physical death if that is our only option for change. A different approach might be called for, one of taking on the dark emptiness or the fiery inferno of that space in the chest and holding it, being both in it and outside it as observer, until it begins to transform; until its loathsome ugliness begins to change.

It took some time before I could embrace the dragon in my chest. Body work of many kinds aided the process. Long after the cough and the fire were gone, my struggles to know the dragon continued to show me firsthand that a major task of coming to age is to acknowledge and embrace our embodiment, our primitive saurian being. This is a vital preparation for old age and death. It means accepting the dragon, with all its scales and lumberings, all its frightful habits, as opposed to denying or aggressively trying to overcome our symptoms, our aches and pains and fears of aging.

Leaving the heroic stance that has historically been the modus operandi of most humans takes considerable conscious awareness and courage, for it often means doing work that is counter to all our learned responses. For women as well as men, heroism that destroys the "bad object" has become the expected response to energies like those of the dragon, that is, any symptom or body response that seems strange, monstrous or frightening. It seldom occurs to us to see meaning in disease.

If we are to be like the princess who kissed the frog, turning him into a prince, or the young prince who embraced the laidly worm, we must come to terms with our relationship to the inner contrasexual, the animus or anima, especially in its dark or monstrous aspects. Like the Celtic Ceridwen, we may want to redeem this dark side of ourselves, only to find that our most careful plans go awry. For those of us in the croning years, something else may be struggling to come into consciousness. We want to redeem our aging, bathe it in the fountain of youth or bask in its great wisdom, but a new task is imposed: growing old and preparing for death. And when we finally swallow the truth, we may become pregnant with a future possibility we could not possibly foresee. It is not easy to accept and experience our aging bodies and psyches without getting caught in a complex that urges us to adopt an heroic stance. Again we seek to turn life around, to redeem all of our failures before we get too old.

We must sacrifice even that desire. Only if we can let the redemption of our darkest fears fail, only if we can give up our brightest hopes, is *metanoia* possible. This means giving up all the collective urgings to perpetuate the patterns of the youthful ego and shadow. When we can willingly sacrifice our old ego goals in all their lightness and darkness of being, then there is a chance for a fuller, more open dialogue between ego and Self.

Within the lungs of the dragon lies the fire of transformation. Dragon fire is primitive affect that has never been expressed, a product of the earthy, undifferentiated animal energy hidden in caves, those openings in the earth that lead to the nether world of archetypal images. One analysand dreamed of such a fire as her own life source that she must protect at all cost from those who would steal it or put it out.

Dragons are guardians of such treasure, protecting it from external and internal forces that would destroy or steal it. The dragon protects the treasure of the true meaning of our embodiment, the joining of *Physis* and *Nous*. If we dwell, imaginally, in its cave or near its body, we are in the liminal space between ego and archetype where the fires of transformation lie banked in the ashes of old attitudes. Here older people struggle to attain the treasure: a new stage of life, a new attitude toward the world and oneself, and the eventual death of one's own dragon body.

If it is dragon energy that keeps our bodies functioning in a healthy fashion, then a connection between this saurian control and our immune system is strong. The immune center is in the hypothalamus, located just behind the breast bone, about in the center of the Kundalini heart chakra, *anahata*. The immune system is seen by psychologists and medical practitioners as the area containing the body's and the psyche's ability to differentiate between what is "me" and what is "not-me"—which cells belong in our bodies and which should be rejected, what contents belong to our psyches and what should be refused as "other."

Many older people have begun to discover that work on the body can open energy channels and invigorate the hypothalamus. We may think of massage as a luxury, but more and more we are realizing that techniques like shiatsu, acupuncture, yoga, breath work and polarity, to name a few, promote a flow of energy and a strengthening of the immune system. Through this kind of work we literally embrace our saurian animal bodies, strengthening and healing our connection with our own flesh and bones.

Even those who do body work, and perhaps particularly those who have long been on the difficult path of individuation, are apt to experience in the late-liminal transition the hot fires that cook up the changes of aging. Before the new attitude reaches consciousness, it must awaken, like Kundalini, and rise from the unconscious. It must be tempered by the fires of passion. And something must be sacrificed before the changes can be embodied. Then the dragon is truly transformed.

In the wisdom of ancient China and Japan, the serpent/dragon was known as a symbol of creativity. Those who were visited by one were considered blessed, and much was expected of them in return. One Japanese legend, "The Vision of Hojo-no-Tokimasa," tells of a visitation in which the serpent's scales were left behind as a sign of protection by a divine force:

> Tokimasa prayed to the goddess Benzaitan for her protection. After three weeks of incessant prayer, Tokimasa was granted a vision of Benzaitan in the form of serpent. As she disappeared, Benzaitan left behind her three serpent scales that were treasured by Tokimasa as a pledge of divine protection.[139]

Jung saw the dragon and snake as symbolic representations of the negative mother, expressions of the "resistance to incest, or the fear of it."[140] We might paraphrase this by saying that the dragon represents our fear of being swallowed and losing ourselves in an incestuous union with the All, the unconscious, the Mother. We must either fight or embrace and transform that dragon—our own perception of our aging bodies—if we are to receive the treasure: greater consciousness and *metanoia*.

It is essential to differentiate between embracing the dragon and being swallowed up in its embrace. Herein lies the value of active imagination. As Jung points out, the voluntary involvement with a fantasy may look like a psychosis, but there is an enormous difference. Rather than being inundated with uncontrollable fantasies as they erupt from the unconscious, voluntary involvement such as active imagination has a purpose:

> To integrate the statements of the unconscious, to assimilate their compensatory content, and thereby produce a whole meaning which alone makes life worth living and, for not a few, possible at all.[141]

Such work can look like psychosis because one is integrating the same kind of fantasy material that can swallow up the insane person. Jung continues:

> In myths the hero is the one who conquers the dragon, not the one who is devoured by it. And yet both have to deal with the same

---

[139] Recounted in A. Hyatt Mayor, ed., *Hokusai*, Metropolitan Museum of Art calendar, 1967.
[140] *Symbols of Transformation*, CW 5, par. 395.
[141] *Mysterium Coniunctionis*, CW 14, par. 756.

dragon. Also, he is no hero who has never met the dragon, or who, if he once saw it, declared afterwards that he saw nothing.[142]

And again:

> It is precisely the strongest and best among men, the heroes, who give way to their regressive longing and purposely expose themselves to the danger of being devoured by the monster of the maternal abyss. But if a man is a hero, he is a hero because, in the final reckoning, he did not let the monster devour him, but subdued it, not once but many times.[143]

It is not that those who take on the task of transforming the dragon are unafraid. Fear is like the bristles of Afaggdu, Ceridwen's dark and unredeemable son, for it protects and armors one. Perhaps awe is a better description, for the ability to embrace our worst fears is truly awe-full.

Doing active imagination around these energies is not easy. It is not a parlor game or a simple technique. It can take us into fiery, archaic depths that challenge the very bone, breath and blood of our being. An alchemical image of such a process shows a woman whose body is held in a grave in the embrace of a great dragon. Both are turning to blood.[144] Images like this are vivid reminders of the power, the terror and the threat to physical being that can be part of the descent into this kind of material. Yet the rewards are great. More and more people are feeling the need to enter the cave of their dragon fears in search of the treasure. More and more are beginning to experience what it is like to embrace the "loathly damosel" rather than slay her in the old, heroic fashion. Both sexes are learning to face the terror and the longing of such work.

In Tarot card spreads there is usually one card that represents both one's hopes and one's fears. Facing the dragon is like this card. Sometimes our hopes can be even more overwhelming than our

---

142 Ibid.

143 "The Relations between the Ego and the Unconscious," *Two Essays on Analytical Psychology,* CW 7, par. 261.

144 Final emblem in Michael Maier's *Scrutinium chymicum,* reproduced in Stanislas Klossowski de Rola, *The Golden Game,* p. 96.

fears. Sarah, an older woman afraid of her own developing role in the world, dreamed:

> I am pinned and paralyzed on a garden bench between Q [a woman who had achieved fame in her later years], and a skinny little old dream-raggedy-man who for years has warned me not to get overextended or inflated. There is a really important task I must perform but I can't move.

Only when she was able to embrace both her hope and her fear of success was she able to escape from the complex that held her fast.

Active imagination in the croning years may carry us more deeply into the psyche than anything we've ever done. This can feel like drowning, as it did for the woman who wrote a poem about herself disintegrating and reintegrating in Ceridwen's kettle. Or it may, as it did for Sarah, bring the image of a trip deep into the ocean depths of the inner life, where profound symbols can bring a new integration of energies and a new understanding of the meaning and purpose of one's life:

> I am swimming underwater when suddenly a great male Orca appears before me and carries me down and down, deeper than I ever imagined I could go. It is enormous, but very beautiful in its black and white colors. I feel that I can only surrender in trust to this force that carries me down. The water we travel through is like viscous air and I have no trouble breathing.
>
> Then this whale brings me to another; a wise old being, a great behemoth, a dragon of the deep, all covered with barnacles and shells which seem to be growing out of his/her withered gray flesh. This whale is monstrously ugly. I know she/he never surfaces, but has lived for millennia down here in the depths. I feel awestruck at the tremendous wisdom emanating from it. Somehow I know that I can choose whether to go slowly down with this enormous being as a guide, or try to find my own way back to the surface. I have the sense that it hopes to show me something at the bottom of the sea, but I must make the choice.
>
> Waking up, I wonder if what I am glimpsing, far below, is my own death. Yet it also seems as if, looking far, far down, I've seen the glow of an ancient treasure which has lain at the bottom of the sea for millennia, protected by this ancient whale.

As we attempt to allow the dissolution of even our most cherished patterns of being, to follow whatever guides us into our own depths, we struggle with the dark and the light energies of both our bodies and the psyche itself. The choices are up to us, but the journeys we make may take us beyond anything our rational minds expect. They may bring us to fear and to feelings of despair. We may feel we're losing our minds, as well as the use of our bodies. We may be forgetful and dissociated. We may lose the sense of who we used to be. But we may also gain a treasure, a richer life.

As we do this, we face not only our greatest fears but also the glimmering hope of a new creativity. The loss of our youthful vigor is one of those dragon fears. Another is the awareness that our bodies are mortal. When we can embrace our terrors and our failures, we also embrace hope for the celebrations to come, when what we have incubated emerges from the underworld.

Legend and myth tell us again and again that transformation is possible. The maiden becomes queen. The dragon becomes prince or princess. The fool becomes wise. The naive attitudes of youth change and develop. Slowly we become ourselves, free to be the keepers of memory and wisdom. We learn when to be silent and when to speak, what can be shared and what is secret. We learn to honor our bodies even as they begin to fail. We come to a visceral understanding of the cycles of change and our part in them.

Ulrich Schaffer writes in his book of poems, *Surprised By Light:*

Again and again the miracle takes place
in the amazing transformation
in which the air turns into leaves
and the earth becomes roots,
in which the sun fills the seed to bursting -
then lets it break open and sprout.
New life breaks through
in the transformation of death.

We are sustained by the surprise of the miracle,
by the change of the seasons,
and I am a link in this miraculous chain.
In me the unchangeable also changes

and I know that I would break
the rhythm of creation
if I did not change.
I would be dead to life
even as I continued to live.

I am not yearning for great miracles,
but for the daily change,
the almost imperceptible rebirth,
the insignificant miracle of growth,
which is greater than all others.[145]

This is the true *metanoia*, an almost imperceptible accumulation of daily change.

---

[145] *Surprised by Light,* p. 6. (Copyright © 1980 by Ulrich Schaffer. Reprinted by permission of HarperCollins, Publishers, Inc.)

7

Becoming Crones

As we grow to appreciate the dragon energy in our late-liminal years, we may also discover the creativity of becoming crones. In similar fashion, as we come to appreciate the crone we may discover a relationship with the Self that affirms our destiny as elders. Whether we recognize some of her characteristics within ourselves or project them onto others, the opportunity to know ourselves more fully can come through our experiences of the crone. Whether her qualities dwell in female bodies or male, respect for the archetypal image of the wise old woman in her many forms can constellate our inner healer. As Marion Woodman writes:

> I have known four or five Crones, two of them men. I have gone to them when I thought I couldn't go any further. Their love was palpable. No advice. Simply being, saying almost nothing. I knew I was totally seen and totally understood. They could constellate my own inner healer because they could see me as I am.[146]

The crone is a pattern imprinted deep within the human psyche. She is the third face of the Triune Goddess, who embodies the fresh possibilities of youth, the productiveness of middle age, and both the deprivation and wise nurturance of old age. Of these three, the crone aspect is perhaps the most powerful. Her face is weathered like old gnarled wood; her penetrating eyes see deep into our souls and beyond to the depths of the universe. Her clawlike fingers appear to reach out and pull us ever closer into her bony embrace—all this both frightens and fascinates. We cannot imagine serving her, yet something at the core of our being knows that this could be one of our greatest creative tasks—to accept and serve the archetypal demands of our own aging.

---

[146] *Conscious Femininity: Interviews with Marion Woodman,* p. 88.

The crone can be challenging, for she carries the opposites: birth-death, youth-age, beauty-ugliness, hope-despair. When we experience these oppositions within ourselves and face the work of their reconciliation in our own lives, we truly do take on what Jung called the *vocation* of developing our personalities right up to the end of life. While this is an exciting challenge at any age, it is particularly strong—frightening as well as creative—for those coming to age. Barbara Hannah reports that when Jung was asked if he thought there would be an atomic war he replied:

> I think it depends on how many people can stand the tension of the opposites in themselves. If enough can, I think we shall escape the worst. But if not, and there is atomic war, our civilization will perish, as so many civilizations have perished before, but on a much larger scale.[147]

The mature person in whom integrity has begun to overcome despair has a unique perspective on the importance of such labor.

In mythology the crone is the archetypal wise old woman. As the "thousand-named goddess," she is known as Tiamat, the birth-giving ocean; Maat, the white feather of truth; Medusa, whose countenance turned men to stone; Fata Morgana, who brought men to their fate; Sophia, highest wisdom; Brigit, who brought the cycles of the seasons; Kali, who destroyed that creation could come into being; and Syrian Mari, who could search the soul. She appears in all these forms and many more. To ancient and contemporary pagans she is the wisest of the wise. To others she is "the whore of Babylon."[148]

By looking at the crone and seeing the opposites within her we may see as if in a mirror the light and dark, good and evil, in ourselves. While we might prefer to deny her dark qualities, it is important to look squarely at both sides if we are to know her reality. Since the crone's shadow side is how she has been known for hundreds of years, and is still known to much of the world today, we might start by looking at her dark aspects.

---

[147] *Encounters with the Soul,* p. 8.
[148] Walker, *The Crone,* p. 68.

To medieval scholars she was the loathsome damosel, "hideous to behold, as if she had been spawned in hell":

> She wears her hair plaited into two short black braids, her neck and hands are black as iron and her eyes small as a rat's. She has a nose like an ape's, lips like a donkey's, teeth like the yoke of an egg and a beard like an ox, to which are added a hump in front and behind and bandy legs. In her hand she carries a scourge.[149]

Begging for connection, yet a monster to those who see only her outer form, she appears to seekers of treasure. Today we resist this gnarled, warted old woman when she comes in dreams and fantasies, feeling only horror at her desire to transform herself and us. We know her from fairy tales as Baba Yaga or the witch. A terror to those who reject or try to manipulate her, she dwells in her hut in the woods of the unconscious, cut off from the conscious world of daily life. Even her name has become a term of opprobrium, calling up images of an old hag who fattens up children only to feed on them herself (certainly an apt mythic description for those who view death as an annihilating end).

As one friend wrote to me:

> I see her as one of those pathetic, isolated, eccentric, beak-nosed widows who lived in the Black Forest on root tea and berries. Crones seem passive to me, frightening to children and vulnerable to the projections of the surrounding society.

The dark crone has long been known as the harbinger of illness and death. Sometimes she brings the psychological death of an old way of being. Like the Tower card in the Tarot deck, our old structures crumble and we fall away from old familiar forms. At other times the crone brings transformation of our physical selves. Our bodies change, our energy for daily living changes; we get thinner or smaller or more arthritic. Our hair turns gray or white. We develop wrinkles. Some of us, like Georgia O'Keefe, start to look like apple dolls. We may lose our teeth or our hair, our ability to concentrate or

---

[149] Emma Jung and Marie-Louise von Franz, *The Grail Legend,* pp. 175-176.

remember. We may turn in on ourselves and forget how to communicate by more than a sigh. This is the horror of the crone. She can rob us of so much.

She can also bring the end of life in the body. As Hecate-Demeter-Persephone, she is gatekeeper at the doors of birth and death. One of the tasks of aging is to prepare ourselves for our own physical death. In the Far East yogins and other wise ones practice their eventual death for many years. Only now is this practice becoming known in the West.[150] In recent decades our generation been encouraged to think about death rather than deny it. Such thoughts still may draw criticism from others.

As death, the crone has the power to destroy. We try to run away, but she pursues. Her eider priestesses are dakinis, "sky walkers" who prepare the dying for their transitions and lead them in spirit form into "the mysterious Land of the Intermediate State."[151] As fate, she brings us messages of our destiny. Often we refuse to listen, but she waits and speaks again. As the agent of change, she is the "Earth-Shaker" who comes out of her cave and shakes her rain stick to alter the world.

In Webster's dictionary crone is defined as "old ewe" and "withered hag." Surely this is the dark shadow side of the aging woman, a perfect screen for our projections of the bad mother. When the breasts sag and wither, they are "bad," unable to give nourishment. When knees get knobby and hips fail, it is hard enough to support ourselves without trying to carry others.

Centuries-long indoctrination limits our imagination so that we see this ancient aspect of the feminine only in her negative forms—loathsome lady, deadly damosel, dreadful dragon. We see her as the one who brings death to our old way of being, to our lives as we have known them, and to our embodied selves. Our fear of the unconscious makes the crone into an image of evil. Fear of the aged Dark Mother who is death or depression often prevents us from accepting

---

[150] See Sogyal Rinpoche, *The Tibetan Book of Living and Dying*.

[151] Walker, *The Crone*, pp. 74-75.

the crone archetype as a source of new creative power. We cannot allow ourselves to realize that the Old Woman or Hag carries the key to success. If we could only see past our fearful perceptions of her outer form, the inner reconciling reality of her containment of the opposites (good-evil, love-hate, beauty-beast) may offer answers to some of our greatest dilemmas. If we could accept her guidance and welcome her wisdom as we age, embracing what appears to be loathsome, we might experience a true *metanoia,* the reconciliation of ego and Self. She is, after all, the midwife of birth as well as death.

As wise woman and keeper of the cauldron, the crone knows the secret of regeneration. Many believe that knowledge of her cycles of death and rebirth have been passed down through generations in spite of a three-century holocaust in which millions of women were killed by persecutors whose fear of the dark unknown became terror of the womb and of the feminine. She is the midwife of death. She is also, as Longfellow writes, "Nature, the old nurse,"[152] who takes the child upon her knee and teaches the secrets of the universe.

Crone should be an honorable term. Even without conscious understanding, generations of men and women have celebrated the rich imagery and symbolism of her dark earthiness and her radiant, numinous moon-light, honoring her cycles of life, death and rebirth as they planted and harvested and planted again. Many feel that originally the crone was so powerful that she was imaged as the female equivalent of the Great Sky Father. As Walker writes:

> The Crone's title was related to the word *crown*, and she represented the power of the ancient tribal matriarch who made the moral and legal decisions for her subjects and descendants. As an embodiment of wisdom, she was supposed to have written the first tablets of the law and punished the first sinners.[153]

The crone is not going to leave us alone once she stirs in us. She seeks creative form; if she can't find it, she may become destructive, causing all sorts of havoc until she is noticed and given space in our

---

152 "The Fiftieth Birthday of Agassiz," in *Longfellow's Poems,* vol 1.
153 *The Crone,* pp. 13-14.

lives. We may experience her destructiveness as a hopeless lethargy. Or we may take on qualities like the sharp-tongued know-it-all who projects discontent onto friends and enemies alike, rather than the meditative or mentoring one we wish to be (what one person calls "the would-be wise").

The truth is that all these qualities are part of the complex we call crone. If we recognize them as such, then we are more able to choose between acting them out and getting to know them in ourselves without identifying with them. When the crone complex does catch us, we may feel as though we're trapped in the icy cold, or, on the contrary, burning to ash with flaming feelings. Either way we need to find a way to give form to what the crone yearns to express in our lives. If we don't give her an outlet, she will continue to be negative in our lives as well as in the way the world perceives her.

Within each of us there is a basic instinct to nurture the spark of life that lies hidden deep within the psyche. Just as the biological instinct drives us toward food and sex, the energy of the archetypes drives us toward creative expression. One man dreamed of the archetypal layer of the psyche as bedrock. A woman dreamed of it as amorphous mists, struggling at dawn to form clouds in the shape of ideas. In many old cultures imagination and the creation of art are as much a part of daily life as eating and sleeping. The weaving of myth, of cloth and of life are all daily tasks. Yet in our "civilized" world imagination and creativity are often considered quite separate from daily activities.

For many in later life the drive to create seems to have atrophied. When menopause and retirement have been left behind, diminishing our abilities and opportunities to parent children of the body or of our will, we may feel our creative energies have also vanished. But they may just lie coiled in the unconscious, only stirring occasionally.

When there is no new creative outlet, ennui can easily bed down in us as well. Our enthusiasm for life seems to vanish. We feel tired and bored, somewhat like the woman who marks her uneventful days by the opening and closing of her curtains. She is adept at activity for its own sake, to keep the feeling of emptiness at bay. She may do all sorts of make-work tasks, but the feeling is still there, just below the surface, like dark winter water under ice. For some, however, coming to age brings up the crone archetype like a boiling volcano. The fires of creativity erupt into consciousness and spew all over the place.

It is our responsibility to find a creative outlet. For one person it might be to start painting, like Grandma Moses, the remembered scenes of childhood. It might involve passing on one's life story to grandchildren, either in writing or telling. It might be working with wood, stone or clay, writing poetry, gardening, volunteer work, returning to school, making new friends or sharing a fresh-eyed wonder at the tiny miracles of nature. I remember a little church in Ogburn St. George, England, where a group of women had done needlepoint kneeling cushions of the story of St. George and the Dragon. Each cushion was a unique labor of love. One even showed something very similar to the *fier baiser*, as if George embraced the dragon rather than destroyed it. There are any number of ways in which we might give form to crone energies.

As I ponder on my own relationship to the crone's creativity, the myth of Demeter and Persephone rises again and again into my mind. At first I ignore it. Demeter is, after all, a mother goddess; producer of all beings, earth mother, corn mother, guardian of birth and fruitfulness. In her myth, told in "The Hymn to Demeter,"[154] she is at the peak of motherhood as her daughter, the Kore, approaches puberty. Demeter also appears to be at the peak of her own creativity. She is certainly an apt image for midlife achievement.

How then can she be seen as a crone? Her images are all of a goddess who lavishes life's bounties upon the world. What has she to do with aging and death? Her anguish when her beloved daughter is abducted into the underworld seems a prototype for the midlife struggle one has when it is time to relinquish motherhood, of physical children and ideas. Nevertheless, something in me kept insisting that Demeter's story was one which could have a great psychological

---

[154] Michael Grant, *Myths of the Greeks and Romans,* pp. 126 ff.

impact on those coming to age. Demeter could speak to us as crone if we would only listen.

As "Triple-goddess," Demeter reaches out to us wherever we are in the life span. If we see her as maiden, the Kore, she shows her youthful form. If we read about her as mother, that is what we perceive. If we look for the crone, we meet Hecate, the ancient one of the crossroads. If we look at all three forms in terms of the liminal years before old age, we can see that all three are one. The crone contains the child and the adult, the maiden and the mother, as well as the old one. Demeter is a woman coming to age whose youthful creativity has suddenly vanished, raped out of daily life by some terrible catastrophe, leaving only despair.

The next and final chapter explores the significance of Demeter for those experiencing or awaiting late-life change. As we shall see, she does embody the crone in all her dark and light aspects. Indeed, in some versions of the myth Demeter herself goes down into the underworld. Thus she is an appropriate psychopomp to guide us in our own descents.

8

Demeter: Myth and Metanoia

To enter into the figure of Demeter means to be pursued, to be robbed, raped, to fail to understand, to rage and grieve, but then to get everything back and to be born again.

—C. Kerényi, *Two Essays on a Science of Mythology.*

The myth of Demeter is a story of sorrow. It is a story of the aridity and anguish an older person feels when his or her creativity has disappeared. Demeter's youthful zest for life is lost, and she has no idea where to begin to search for it. Only Hecate, her ancient feminine wisdom, her "moon consciousness," hears her lament. Only Hecate suspects that her precious potential has been carried off into the underworld, the realm of Zeus-Hades, the dark chaotic depths of the unconscious.

The myth of Demeter describes a time of total devastation in the life of a goddess of ancient Greece. It is a story of what happens when the nurturing, creative qualities of a person coming to age are torn away by life events or inner vocation, caught between the opposites of the status quo and the demanding forces of change. It spoke to the souls of people in ancient times and was the basis of their religious practice for over fifteen hundred years. If we listen, it may speak again today when the myths that honor age are all but forgotten. Suppose that we find in Demeter a figure who magnifies our own journeys through the late-liminal years and carries our projections of grief and hope.

Suppose we enter into this image in search of ourselves.

The Myth

Demeter was the beautiful daughter of Rhea and Cronus. Cronus swallowed his children at birth so that none could replace him as high god. Demeter came into the world when her brother Zeus tricked their father Cronus into vomiting up his children. Zeus indeed banished and replaced the father, then married Hera, another sister, who became his queen. But he coveted the beauty of Demeter. When she refused his advances, he took on his bull form and raped her. The offspring of that rape was a daughter, the Kore (usually pronounced Kor-eh, meaning the maiden), a golden child of great promise whom her mother loved most tenderly. Their love for one another brought the whole world into bloom.

One day the maiden went alone to a great meadow filled with blossoms to gather flowers for her beloved mother. There she spied a triple-blossomed narcissus that was so beautiful she fell into a rapture looking at it. She didn't notice the earth opening up behind her. Too late she felt the grip of her uncle, Hades, king-god of death and the underworld. She cried out in terror as he snatched her up and carried her off to his domain.

Some say that no one heard her cries. Others say her pleas were heard only by the old hermit goddess Hecate in the darkness of her cave, silent and withdrawn from the affairs of the world. They say that the maiden's abduction was seen only by Helios, the earth's sun, who could not intervene. Heard or unheard, seen or unseen, the deed was done. Demeter was bereft, all joy ripped from her life, her only purpose a seemingly useless search for her lost child. Dressed in the rags and ashes of mourning, the aging mother wandered the earth, utterly despondent, begging news of her beloved daughter.

Her despair deepening, her creativity lost with the child, Demeter wandered a long, long time and eventually came to the town of Eleusis. Here she leaned against a well at the center of the village, consumed with grief and exhaustion. Here the king's daughters, coming for water, found her. Taking pity on the exhausted old woman, they took her home to their royal mother who needed a nurse for her baby son. This mother's name was Metaneira (possibly from *metanoia,* and thus foreshadowing a great change). Offered every good thing to eat and drink, Demeter would have nothing except a few sips of barley water, a cooling drink that the reapers drank at harvest time and that later became the sacred drink at Eleusis. She would drink only the reaper's cup, perhaps to emphasize her own harvest of sorrow.

Like Isis in her grieving search for her lost mate Osiris, Demeter in her grief took on the guise of an old woman and the role of nurse. Her own creativity gone, she tried to create a substitute by making Metaneira's child immortal. Nightly she placed the boy, Demophoön, into a holy fire until her efforts were interrupted by the terrified shrieks of the mother, whereupon Demeter dropped the baby and furiously revealed herself in all her blinding glory. Unlike most humans who are burned to ashes by such *numen*, Metaneira survived to atone for interrupting the goddess's rite. She oversaw the building of an altar and temple where she became priestess of the rites Demeter demanded.

Meantime Demeter sought out Hecate in the isolation of her cave and was told of her child's terrified cries. Then, when Hecate sent her to Helios, she finally learned of her Kore's fate, carried off to the land of the dead, "the formless, unsubstantial realm of Hades."[155] Rage came up in Demeter and spilled out upon the land, bringing illness, infertility and death to all growing things. No plants, animals or humans could give birth. No creative act could take place. The whole world became barren, killed by the searing breath of Demeter's fury.

That year was the cruelest humankind had ever known. There was famine in all the earth. Demeter's devastation would have wiped out the whole human race had not the high god Zeus finally intervened, afraid that soon there would be no humans left to worship the gods. Zeus commanded his brother Hades to release Queen Persephone to return to her mother. Knowing that he must obey, Hades reluctantly let her go. But first he tempted her with a juicy pomegranate. Warned never to eat or drink in the underworld but so thirsty she was unable to resist, Persephone put just one seed into her mouth. Even as she

---

155 Carl Kerényi and C.G. Jung, *Two Essays on a Science of Mythology: The Myths of the Divine Child and the Divine Maiden*, p. 124.

sprang into her mother's arms with joy, Persephone had to confess that she had tasted the sacred fruit of the underworld and sexuality. She had joined with Hades and become his queen, bound to him by the brief quenching of her own desire. Thus Demeter learned that her daughter must return in endless cycles of rebirth to the domain beneath the earth she now ruled with Hades.

After the reunion between mother and daughter, Zeus sent Rhea, their mother and Persephone's grandmother, to appeal to Demeter to make the earth fruitful again and to return once more to her place among the gods on Mt. Olympus. Soon the grain was tall and the whole earth burst forth with life, but Demeter would not return to her former post on the heights until she had taught humankind

> awful mysteries which no one may . . . transgress or pry into or utter, for deep awe of the gods checks the voice. Happy is [one] . . . on earth who has seen these mysteries; his lot will be good in the world to come. But to him who is uninitiated . . . such good things do not befall once he is dead, down in the darkness and gloom.[156]

At last Demeter, with Persephone beside her for part of each year, went to dwell on Olympus among her kin, those

> "deathless gods," far removed from suffering mortals destined to die. . . . In their grief, and at the hour of death, men could turn for compassion to the goddess who sorrowed and the goddess who died.[157]

Demeter's loss of her daughter into the underworld echoes age-old stories of the cycle of descent and return. One of the oldest is the tale of Inanna's journey down through seven gates to the underworld where she is stripped to her bones before reemerging.[158] In the myth of Demeter, Persephone went down a virginal maiden and emerged a royal queen. Raped from her former naive state, she was condemned to a cycle of eternal return. This was both the curse and the blessing of Persephone, as well as the anguish and joy of Demeter.

---

156 Grant, *Myths of the Greeks and Romans,* p. 96.

157 Edith Hamilton, *Mythology: Timeless Tales of Gods and Heroes,* p. 54.

158 For a psychological perspective on the Inanna myth, see Sylvia Brinton Perera, *Descent to the Goddess: A Way of Initiation for Women.*

When the earth shall bloom with the fragrant flowers of spring in every kind, then from the realm of darkness and gloom you shall come up once more to be a wonder for gods and mortal men.[159]

Demeter and Persephone in Our Lives Today

In the years of retirement and change, many of us feel pursued, robbed and raped by life events and inner turmoil. When the loss of a job or significant others plunges us into despair, we enter into the image of Demeter, experiencing her anguish. Both the lost one and the loser, we long for what has vanished but have little hope of recovering it without assistance. The world is drying up around us, and we can only mourn in confusion. Our minds wander in strange places as we search for answers.

Eventually we may take on a new project, attempting to replace what is missing. We travel, study, meditate, seek spiritual guidance. No matter how many temples we build or rites we conduct, either in our psyches or in the world, we are still apt to go through a period of mourning as we face our fears of coming to age. Then we feel that our creative juices have dried up. One older analysand said to me recently, "When you figure out a formula for becoming creative as you age, please pass it on to me."

But there is no formula. We can't know what to do about this stage of our lives. Like Demeter, we search for an answer, hoping for divine intervention. Eventually we may turn inward, searching out the mythic Hecate, seeking the crone-hermit within who holds the lantern of what Erich Neumann calls moon consciousness.[160] This dim light can point the way toward Helios, our bright sun awareness. Then we discover the truth. We have lost our youth and no matter how hard we try we can't get it back. Like the woman who fell asleep by the highway and lost her petticoats, we are irrevocably changed. How, then, do we live? In place of a formula for recovering our former creativity, it might help to go further into the myth.

---

[159] Grant, *Myths of the Greeks and Romans,* pp. 127-128.
[160] "The Moon and Matriarchal Consciousness," p. 50.

Demeter's name in Greek is De, meaning delta, the triangle that represents her triple-goddess form. Some scholars feel that the delta on ancient pots and cult objects represents the sacred vulva of the goddess and thus a doorway to the mysteries.[161] When we are undergoing a vestibule experience, we stand between the old and the new with one door closed behind and the one ahead as yet unopened. We are in Demeter's doorway, that place under the lintel between two worlds. One is "our world, the world in which our sun shines," and the other is "the world before and outside creation . . . [where] all things have their source."[162]

Demeter's doorway opens to the sacred mysteries that took place in the womb of earth and led to the beyond, traditionally seen as ruled by Hades who was then the lord of death.[163] The lintel of the huge doorway into Agamemnon's tomb in Mycenae is built in the triangular shape of her delta. Men and women alike were admitted to her mysteries. The Greek word *meter* means mother. Thus Demeter is the mother-goddess of earth and the feminine. She is also three: the maiden, the mother and the crone.

A goddess triad was known long before Demeter. Kerényi reports that in ancient Arcadia Hera, mother of the gods, had three forms: maiden, fulfilled woman and woman of sorrows. Thus, he reminds us, Demeter figures always contain their own maiden form as well as the crone Hecate, the Moon Goddess, whom Kerényi calls "the *double of Demeter, herself.* "[164] He goes on:

> The budlike idea of the connection between three aspects of the world—maiden, mother and moon—hovers at the back of the triad of goddesses in the Homeric hymn. . . . The poet of the *Theogeny* [Hesiod] acclaims her as the mighty Mistress of *three* realms—earth, heaven and sea.[165]

---

[161] See Barbara Walker, *The Woman's Encyclopedia of Myths and Secrets,* p. 218.

[162] Carl Kerényi, *Eleusis: Archetypal Image of Mother and Daughter,* p. 33.

[163] It is important to distinguish Hades from Satan, the latter being lord of evil whereas Hades was lord of the underworld.

[164] Kerényi and Jung, *Two Essays on a Science of Mythology,* p. 110.

[165] Ibid., p. 112.

Like the Hermit/Crone of the Tarot deck, Hecate carries a lantern to show the way. Hecate is called "bringer of light," mistress of the spirits. She, too, has three faces.[166] There is some question about whether or not it is she who contains the other two (Demeter and Kore), even though later myths, like the "Hymn to Demeter," made her the least important, barely mentioning her name. It makes sense to us as we age that the crone contains the maiden and the matron, just as our own lives contain all that has gone before. Kerényi describes them:

A compact group, a triad of unmistakable individuals, this is how the hymn shows the three goddesses: Mother, Daughter, and the moon goddess Hecate. They are easily confused on sacred monuments, because the torch appears to be the attribute of each....

. . . The Greeks attached the name "Hecate" to a goddess who united in herself affinities with the moon, a Demetrian nature, and Kore-like characteristics . . . .

The classical figure of Hecate stands stiff and strange in the Greek world, built up on a triangle, and with faces turned in three directions. They tried to get rid of the stiffness of these Hecate statues by breaking up the triune goddess into three dancing maidens.[167]

Kerényi tells us that in other versions of the myth Hecate too goes to the underworld in search of Persephone, either alone or in the company of Demeter.[168]

Demeter's own mother was Rhea and her grandmother Gaea. All three were goddesses of the earth and its bounty.[169] Cronus, Demeter's father, is better known to most of us today by his Roman name, Saturn. It is he who gives shape and form by establishing boundaries and rules. Thus the unlimited abundance of the nurturing mother and the form-giving restriction of the shaping father came together to produce divine offspring, among them Demeter and her brothers Zeus and Hades.

---

[166] Kerényi, *Eleusis,* p. 64.
[167] Kerényi and Jung, *Two Essays on a Science of Mythology,* pp. 110ff.
[168] Ibid.
[169] *New Larousse Encyclopedia of Mythology,* p. 150.

All three were children of divine violence and banishment. Their grandfather, Uranus, progenitor of all earth, had been mutilated and banished by his son Cronus. (From the dripping blood of the mutilation, the Furies and monstrous giants were born.) Cronus in his turn swallowed all of his children and would not let them live to replace him. He maintained the status quo by refusing to allow any new possibility to come into being, retaining all power within himself.

Through trickery and with the help of his mother, the boy Zeus escaped this fate and lived to purge his father of all he had swallowed. Zeus then cast Cronus into the depths of the universe, replacing him as ruler of the gods on Mt. Olympus much as Cronus had replaced his own father, Uranus. Hades, Cronus's other son, became ruler of the underworld. Cronus had carried the opposites of light and dark, life and death undifferentiated and unrealized within himself. Now he was replaced, and the split between the upper and lower worlds of the gods was accomplished. Zeus was still the higher god and had jurisdiction over his brother, but a new awareness was coming into being with the realization that there was more than one domain in the kingdom of the gods.

And where did Demeter fit into this design? What was her role? She too was royal, and as the myth begins she rules over the earth that lies between and connects the upper and lower kingdoms. The earth and all living things are her domain, as they were for her mother and grandmother before her. Like the earth itself, her severe beauty is coveted by her brother. How can he, grand in his role as high god, resist trying to rule her, too?

Demeter's male relatives all seem to precipitate change by means of mutilation and banishment. Her own transformation and that of her female clan frequently begins with rape and abduction. Change is forced on them. Such a force is often felt in the human psyche today by both men and women. New energies come into conscious awareness through violent occurences that involve severe loss. The "old king," our dominant conscious attitude, is mercilessly battered by life events and something new takes over. We may feel as if we're being ripped apart, the meaning of our lives torn away. Or we may feel raped as new forces ruthlessly penetrate the defenses of old ruling complexes. Often this brings a violent awareness of what has been repressed, and we go through a period of intense rage or grief before accepting a new attitude.

As we go through the meanderings of our own late-liminal crossings, there seems little hope of a creative outcome. Like Demeter, it seems that we will wander aimlessly forever. We look for a solution in books. We ask others for their wisdom, and yet the lostness continues. We are frightened and disoriented, unsure whether taking up golf or going on a trip, or indeed doing anything at all, can give us what we need.

We may immerse ourselves in someone else's project, trying to "fire it" with our energies. If we can't reconnect with our own creativity, at least we can support someone else's. We may help others to prepare themselves for a transforming experience. But this is no substitute for one's own individuation. If parents don't live out their own lives, they often unconsciously influence their children to do it for them. Similarly, if we don't work on our own process, those we seek to help may be subtly pushed to live out our dreams rather than their own. As with Demophoön, this is doomed to failure. Something screams in horror and snatches the "child" away.

To search like Demeter/Hecate for what is lost is a profound task, especially for people growing older. When the search is conducted within the vessel of analysis, it means keeping track of dreams, regularly attending sessions and monitoring one's responses in body and psyche. It requires acquiescing to a process that reduces the available energy for outer activity as libido flows inward. It also means something more. Neumann writes that in Demeter's finding and reuniting with Persephone, the transformative character of the feminine is expressed in the experience of growing from girlhood to womanhood:

> Rape, victimization, downfall as a girl, death, and sacrifice stand at the center of these events, whether they are experienced through the impersonal god, the paternal uroboros, or, as later, personalized and placed in relation to a male who is in every sense "alien."

But Kore is not merely overcome by the male; her adventure is in the profoundest sense a self-sacrifice, a being-given-to-womanhood, to the Great Goddess as the female self. Only when this has been perceived or emotionally suffered and experienced in the mystery, has the *heuresis,* the reunion of the young Kore turned woman, with Demeter, the Great Mother, been fulfilled. Only then has the Feminine undergone a central transformation, not so much by becoming a woman and a mother, and thus guaranteeing earthly fertility and the survival of life, as by achieving union on a higher plane with the spiritual aspect of the Feminine, the Sophia aspect of the Great Mother, and thus becoming a moon goddess.[170]

When we can be faithful to our descents and the turning inward of our energy, choosing to sacrifice our old ways, our feminine energy does undergo a radical transformation. We are no longer held fast in a father complex, but begin to hear with new ears the saturnine inner voice that judges and criticizes. We begin to recognize the one who swallows all the emerging possibilities of our changing lives. Slowly the relationship between ego and Self begins to shift. New attitudes and ideas begin to emerge.

And when the Kore in us begins to change, we find ourselves more aware and more accepting of the transformation and impregnation that goes on when our energy is allowed to gestate in the rich darkness of what feels like defeat and despair. The Kore goes down a child and comes back an adult. She has finally grown up enough to take her own place in relation to the gods. This process is also described in a Biblical passage from Paul's letter to the Ephesians:

That we *henceforth* be no more children, tossed to and fro, and carried about with every wind of doctrine, by the sleight of men, *and* cunning craftiness, whereby they lie in wait to deceive;

But speaking the truth in love, may grow up into him in all things, which is the head, *even* Christ.[171]

For Jung, Christ was most importantly a symbol of the Self.[172] To grow into a person in union with the feminine, to become one

---

[170] *The Great Mother: An Analysis of the Archetype*, p. 319.
[171] Ephesians 4:14-15 (King James version).
[172] See *Aion*, CW 9ii, pars. 68ff.

who has grown closer to the androgyny of the Christ-Self, means that one is no longer a child in the old sense of being naive and virginal. No longer unopened, the individual emerges from the unconscious carrying the new possibilities found in the descent.

In some versions of the Demeter myth, Persephone is pregnant when she returns. This child was conceived when she tasted the seed of the pomegranate, the metaphor for sexuality. Persephone thus discovers herself a woman. Her child is Dionysus born again as Dionysus Zagreus.[173] She comes up bearing consciousness of the power of dissolution and descent. Zagreus was originally a divinity who welcomed the souls of the dead into the underworld and helped with their purification. When the two gods were joined and became Dionysus Zagreus, Dionysus was changed from "the rustic god of wine and jollity . . . the god of orgiastic delirium," to what Plutarch describes as "the god who is destroyed, who disappears, who relinquishes life and then is born again."[174]

Persephone thus comes up bearing not only laughter, ecstasy and the joy life can offer after we are ripened, trodden and aged into wine, but also the knowledge that there is rebirth, in a new form, of what has been lost. Neumann tells us:

> The fruit of her [the Kore's] transformative process becomes the luminous son, the divine spirit-son, spiritually conceived and spiritually born, whom she holds on her lap, or who is handed up to her by the creative Earth Mother aspect. . . . Thus the woman experiences her power to bring forth light and spirit, to generate a luminous spirit that despite changes and catastrophes is enduring and immortal. . . . For in the mystery, she who gives birth renews herself. . . . In the mystery the late psychological insight that matriarchal consciousness was the true native soil of the processes of spiritual growth becomes the "knowledge" of the woman.[175]

Such psychological insight can also become the knowledge of the man who experiences the power of the feminine triad within his life.

---

[173] Kerényi and Jung, *Two Essays on a Science of Mythology,* p. 145.
[174] *New Larousse Encyclopedia of Mythology*, p. 160.
[175] *The Great Mother,* p. 320.

Dionysus can be conceived in the psyche of both genders, just as both can experience the rape, the descent and the consent of Kore-Persephone in their individuation. Men coming to age may wander and mourn and search, caught in the myth of Demeter, much as women do. With support of one kind or another, many return with a new perspective on life. This can happen spontaneously. It can happen in a moment of vision or it can happen slowly, almost invisibly. Pain takes us down. We spend time in the depths, carried off by forces in the psyche that the Greeks named as gods. The one who carries us down is Hades. The one who mourns the loss is Demeter. The one who calls us back, albeit reluctantly, is Zeus.

Over the doorway of Jung's house in Küsnacht is a Latin quotation that means "Called or not called, the god appears." When these archetypal forces come, they initiate us into a mythic story, a mythic milieu. Demeter's story takes us into such mythos. It speaks to us of youth, middle age and old age. It speaks to us about the pain of our losses and the hope of transformation.

A Modern Demeter

Marion was pain-filled and floundering when she came to me for analysis. She didn't know the myth of Demeter, but like the goddess she was experiencing loss and descent. Her enjoyment of life had been carried off. The anguish caused by outer events had gone into her body and psyche so that she thought she was suffering from a fatal disease or going mad. She had fought her depression as hard as she could, but still she was on the edge of total collapse.

Married at twenty to Ken, twelve years her senior, Marion had raised five children, cared for an enormous house and garden with little outside help, and spent many hours doing research for her scientist husband. While Ken had always taken good care of the family's financial needs (Marion had never balanced a check book or paid a bill), he had been either physically or emotionally absent through most of their marriage, unable because of his own history to stay in close relationship.

When Marion was fifty-eight her husband suffered a fatal heart attack. Within the year following his death, both her parents also died. Her children grown and gone, Marion was left alone in a big house and "a big empty life." She became extremely anxious about her own physical well-being. She felt "spacey" and "disconnected," unable to remember names or engagements. Often she would start a task and then lose track of what she was doing. She began to obsess about having Alzheimer's and dying. Repeatedly she had intense rectal pain along with the sensation that her insides were falling out. Often this was followed by such extreme fatigue she could hardly drag herself out of bed. She stopped going out. She stopped eating. When her children came to visit they were shocked by her deterioration and insisted she see the family doctor.

Medical tests uncovered only minor ailments. Her doctor tried to reassure her, explaining that she was suffering a classic grief reaction along with some of the normal debilities of age. He recommended vitamins and a well known tranquilizer "to get her over the hump."

Most days she forgot to take the vitamins. The tranquilizer only seemed to deepen her feeling that she was living in a twilight world waiting for death. Often she spent the day in her bathrobe, wandering about the house aimlessly, telling herself that she must get out and be active, yet unable to choose what dress to put on or where to go. Her mind played tricks. She would hear her husband's car pull into the driveway and the back door open. She could almost catch a glimpse of him coming around the corner of the hall.

When her condition continued to deteriorate and the most sophisticated medical tests produced only negative results, her doctor recommended psychotherapy. At first Marion wouldn't listen. No one in her family had ever had to seek outside help with their personal problems. Surely she was strong enough to get through this on her own. "I guess I've always seen myself as Wonder Woman," she said in our initial interview. "Nothing has ever daunted me before. But now I'm lost. I feel increasingly invisible, as if I'm just fading away to nothing."

In the early sessions she couldn't even cry. All her affect seemed to be locked away. She was certainly experiencing a grief response, but its prolongation indicated that something else had been triggered by her loss. She seemed to be living in a half-world where most of her libido was in the unconscious, unavailable to her outer life.

My work with Marion was one of the seeds of this book. Struggling to stay with her in her pain, I began to realize how little we knew about the symptoms or the tasks of this time of late-life loss in which she felt so alienated from her old life and familiar self. Only my understanding of gerontology and the Jungian concept of honoring the defense, no matter how dysfunctional it might appear, gave me the courage to stay with the apparent destruction. Her fear of that destruction held her fast in a dark underworld filled with paralyzing specters.

Marion was searching for relief from her symptoms and a return of her energy, but the retentiveness in her process was causing her to have anal spasms, both physically and psychologically. She just couldn't let go. I looked for something that might guide us beyond the early anamnesis. Her physical symptoms began to take on new significance. It seemed that she was struggling to find herself, the child of her new way of life still lost in the unconscious but now the focus of a search aided by Hecate's moonlight.

It was some time before she could acknowledge that not only her husband's death, but also her fear of the future and of the changes she must undergo to live without his or her parents' protection had paralyzed her, plunging her into hopelessness and despair. Transformation was now demanded, but the only change she could imagine was illness and death. At one point she felt so faded and invisible that I strongly feared she would follow her husband into the grave. It was anguish for us both. She could not seem to allow herself to anticipate a future. Then she had a dream:

> My mother is outside hunting for a child who is lost. It's dark, but there's a sliver of moon. I see my father looking out the window, but he doesn't come out or help. It's almost as if he has an idea where to look, but he won't. He's just waiting to see what happens. My mother hunts all over, looking and calling. I see her start to go

into the woods. I want to yell and tell her not to. You're not supposed to go in there. Someplace in there the child could be trapped or held captive.

Marion's resistance made it impossible to work directly on the dream material. Instead, I encouraged her to read the Demeter-Persephone myth. She immediately saw parallels between Demeter's search for her lost child and her own dream. This marked a turning point in our work. As she became more involved with the myth, she uncovered long-buried memories of her life with a detached, godly, autocratic father whom she both adored and feared. He and her husband had seen to all her physical needs, but had repeatedly treated her as an extension of themselves. Only long after both of them had died could she slowly begin to realize how much of her life had been lived as a maiden in their care.

In the dream her father, though detached, seems to have a sense of what is going on. Often the father in dreams represents the dreamer's conscious attitude. This seemed to be true in Marion's case, for until then she had been unable to fully involve herself in the analytic work. It was as if her masculine energy, her animus, was an observer rather than a participant.

As a small girl, Marion had had to become almost too good to be true in order to care for her parents' needs. Her mother had been ill through much of Marion's childhood. In her sixties she was still struggling to be their "golden child," the good girl who made everything okay. The death of her husband and her parents was devastating. She hadn't been able to save them. Her guilt at their deaths had symbolically driven the good little girl into a dark place of despair. Marion's enthusiasm for life was lost along with that golden child. Her old unconscious contentment and trust in God had been banished by her pain and anger. She felt like the Kore-maiden, wrested from the happiness of her former life. But even more she felt like Demeter who grieved the loss and wandered the world in search of her maiden self.

Who was that bright, enraptured child, so lost in the narcissus flower that she never saw her fate looming up? All of us, as we come to age, are called to answer this question. Who is the bright child within us, innocent and narcissistic, who is suddenly snatched away as the years pass? For Marion it was the good little girl. It didn't matter that this was a "false-self" created by her parent's narcissistic needs. Without that identity Marion felt dead. She wanted her innocence back.

We've all seen the innocence and healthy narcissism of the three or four year old. I remember one little girl who learned to jump from one stair to another while her mother visited with a friend. "Look at ME, Mommy," she kept calling, "Look at ME!" Her delight in herself and her achievement was contagious. Her sense of herself as the center of her world was lovely. Fortunately her mother was able to interrupt her adult conversation to affirm the child's glorious celebration of herself.

Growing up and seeing ourselves as one among many naturally diminishes that wonder at our own achievement. Often when we put the needs of others first, as Marion learned to do, we never realize how undeveloped this leaves us until some traumatic event penetrates our bubble of contentment. We may be well into our croning years before we are challenged to find our own Persephone. That is one reason why, as we age, we may feel so invisible and cut off from the outer collective. This child within is more than just the child of our past, more than simply the one our parents desired and influenced. Trauma carries the child of our outgrown past off into the unconscious where she is changed in the underworld of despair. Like Persephone, the child becomes a woman and the woman a queen. When she returns the whole world blossoms. She comes carrying the child of the future.

We've all read one article after another about "the inner child" and how to recover, heal or transform this part of ourselves. Such writing is about reclaiming the actual child we once were, before being damaged by some twist of fate. Is this what we seek as we search for what is lost or missing from our lives? Certainly the healing of the personal wounded child can be enormously freeing, but is this what Persephone and her child represent?

Jung wrote of "the divine child":

> Lay prejudice is always inclined to identify the child motif with the
> concrete experience "child". . . . In psychological reality, however,
> the empirical idea "child" is only the means (and not the only one)
> by which to express a psychic fact that cannot be formulated more
> exactly. Hence by the same token the mythological idea of the child
> is emphatically not a copy of the empirical child but a *symbol*
> clearly recognizable as such: it is a wonder-child, a divine child . . .
> and not—this is the point—a human child.[176]

> One of the essential features of the child motif is its futurity. The
> child is potential future. Hence the occurrence of the child motif in
> the psychology of the individual signifies as a rule an anticipation of
> future developments . . . . The "child" paves the way for a future
> change of personality. In the individuation process, it anticipates the
> figure that comes from the synthesis of conscious and unconscious
> elements in the personality. It is therefore a symbol which unites the
> opposites; a mediator, bringer of healing, that is, one who makes
> whole.[177]

For Marion the future held no hope without her parents and husband who had given meaning to her life. When we first started our
work she could not imagine any promise of future developments. It
was winter in her psyche and nothing grew. Over and over I won-
dered if it might not he wise to send her for medication. Over and
over I felt like Gaea, the old grandmother, the seducer's accom-
plice,[178] ruthlessly allowing the maiden to be carried down into her
own transformation, whatever form that might take.

It took a long time for Marion to feel a sense of possibility for her
future. She had to begin by accepting the deaths of her parents, her
husband, and herself as the good little girl. She also had to accept her
own guilt, pain and anger. Like Demeter she searched and raged and
tried substitutes. She began to struggle with her own mortality and to
wonder how she would face her own death when it came.

---

[176] "The Psychology of the Child Archetype," *The Archetypes and the
Collective Unconscious,* CW 9i, par. 273, note 21.
[177] Ibid., par. 278.
[178] See Kerényi and Jung, *Two Essays on a Science of Mythology,* p. 136.

Slowly she emerged from her depression. Eventually she moved into a home that better suited her needs. For the first time in her life she began to paint and took great pleasure in her efforts. While not denying her losses, her focus began to shift to new-found strengths. She knew now that she could survive dark times, recognizing that new life gestated in the darkness. For the first time she began to examine her life and was rewarded by feeling a new sense of herself and her own creativity along with the courage to face the future. Her life now echoed Jung's words after his own late-life trials, regarding "how important it is to affirm one's own destiny."[179]

Marion had, indeed, begun to affirm her destiny. The pain in her rectum was gone. The incomprehensible things that had happened had nearly broken her, but in the end and with the help of therapy, she had endured. When Marion first came to me, she seemed a child. As I watched her develop, especially after the dream of the lost child, it was striking to see the changes in her face, her bearing and her self-confidence. By the time we ended our work together I could see not only the child in her but the mother and the crone as well. She had let her hair show its natural silver color. Her voice, originally high pitched and breathy, had developed a more confident timbre. Body work had helped her become more comfortable in her own skin; she moved with more freedom and less self-consciousness. Her life was not easy. Sometimes she was very lonely. Occasionally she still experienced panic at the thought of being alone in old age.

Recently I received a note from Marion giving me permission to use her material in this book. The importance of her involvement with Demeter seems clear in her words.

I hope you can make some sense out of what went on in those years we worked together. I was so far down in the underworld so much of the time that it's hard for me to put it all together even now. I only know that I lost a part of myself, that I mourned like Demeter and felt as old as Hecate. I guess what means the most to me now, though, is Persephone. It's as if I learned some mystery when all this happened. I learned that when something dies it changes and

---

179 See above, p. 42.

then comes back again in a new form. This doesn't happen just once, either, does it? It happens again and again and again. It's like painting the same scene over and over. Each time it's different. My life is really different now. The same old ups and downs, but somehow they don't get to me like they used to. I know it's a cycle. Sometimes I feel really old. But today I feel pregnant! I have to go because I'm painting.

Marion's *metanoia* was her own. It was not an imitation of Jung's or of the women he loved. It did not fit gerontological theory. Most of the time it didn't seem to fit any theory at all. Yet she left her old ways and attitudes and moved on in her own fashion and with her own results. The myth of Demeter, Hecate and Persephone became more than an active imagination for her. It provided a framework for what she was experiencing. It gave meaning to her losses and hope for recovery from despair.

Many people coming to age have similar experiences.

Anne, a woman in transition, dreamed that she had left her daughter behind, wrapped in a tattered quilt, sobbing in a corner of their old house. Only after she had recovered this child could she truly give herself to what lay ahead.

Gordon, seventy, recovering from the break-up of a romance that had promised to lift him out of a depression, walked down a hill in his home town watching a beautiful sunset. Suddenly it came to him that *metanoia* did indeed mean on-going change, not only of himself but of all his late-life dreams and expectations. In that moment, as he struggled to come to terms with the agony of his sacrifice, he began to accept the war going on in his soul. He knew he would survive and that he could live with his fate, even when it did not contain the "great love" of his life. He realized that he had been offered a more difficult and demanding challenge. He reported that in that instant a great shift took place internally. His defeat had changed to a victory over depression and despair. Nothing external had changed, but he had reclaimed himself and his life.

Such experiences have affirmed my belief that Jung's concept of *metanoia* is just as applicable to late-life transformation as it is to the changes that take place in midlife. Those of us in that transition have an important task ahead of us—to explore and experience the years of our late fifties and sixties in a way that can open our understanding of the trials and triumphs people go through as they come to age. This involves a struggle to recognize the opposites—good-evil, conscious-unconscious, hope-despair, youth-age—within ourselves, our bodies and our world.

At first we may swing like a pendulum from one extreme to the other, feeling torn apart by the tension. Part of the aging process seems to be the desire to connect with the reconciling energy that steadies those extremes—the energy derived from what Jung called the transcendent function. When this reconciliation happens, we become more conscious of how oppositions play themselves out in everyday life. We may also find ourselves at a balance point where we have moments of feeling still and at peace.

People who struggle to go through the transition of their fifties and sixties with an increase of consciousness often become reconciled with their long and sometimes painful history, knowing that it has tempered their spirits and shaped their lives and that it will continue to do so as long as they live. This happened to Gordon, as it has to many others. Coming consciously to age, they know the little deaths of their descents and the rebirths of their returns.

When we realize that we are part of a cycle that periodically draws us down into the darkness of unconsciousness, and then brings us back again into the light where we can blossom, we start to know ourselves in a new way. Coming to age then becomes an exciting exploration, opening the way to our future in this life and beyond.

Bibliography

Berry, Patricia. "What's the Matter with Mother?" In *Fathers and Mothers.* Ed. P. Berry. Zürich: Spring Publications, 1990.

Butler, R. *Why Survive?: Being Old in America.* New York: Harper and Row, 1975.

Callahan, Daniel. *Setting Limits: Medical Goals in an Aging Society.* New York: Simon and Schuster, 1987.

Claremont de Castillejo, Irene. *Knowing Woman: A Feminine Psychology.* New York: G.P. Putnam's Sons, 1967.

Coomaraswamy, Ananda K., "On The Loathly Bride." In *Speculum,* vol. 20, no. 4 (October 1945).

Cumming, Elaine, and Henry, William. *Growing Old: The Process of Disengagement.* New York: Basic Books, 1961.

Doress, Paula; Siegel, Diana; and The Midlife and Older Women Book Project. *Ourselves Growing Older: Women Aging with Knowledge and Power.* New York: Simon and Schuster, 1987.

Edinger, Edward F. *The Creation of Consciousness: Jung's Myth for Modern Man.* Toronto: Inner City Books, 1983.

Erikson, Erik. *Childhood and Society.* New York: W.W. Norton & Company, Inc., 1950.

Ford, Patrick, trans. and ed. *The Mabinogi and Other Medieval Welsh Tales.* Los Angeles: UCLA Press, 1977.

Gilligan, Carol. *In a Different Voice: Psychological Theory and Women's Development.* Cambridge: Harvard University Press, 1982.

Gimbutas, Marija. *The Goddesses and Gods of Old Europe: Myths and Cult Images.* Hampshire: B.A.S. Printers, 1974.

Gordon, Rosemary. *Dying and Creating: A Search for Meaning.* London: Society of Analytical Psychology, 1978.

Gould, Roger. "Transformational Tasks in Adulthood." In *The Course of Life: Psychoanalytic Contributions Toward an Understanding of Personality Development; Vol. 3, Adulthood and Aging.* Ed. Stanley Greenspan and George Pollock. Maryland: U.S. Dept. of Health and Human Services, 1981.

Grant, Michael. *Myths of the Greeks and Romans.* New York: Signet, 1962.

Greene, Anita. "Giving the Body Its Due." In *Quadrant*, vol. 17, no. 2 (Fall 1984).

Gutmann, Daniel. "Psychoanalysis and Aging: A Developmental View." In *The Course of Life: Psychoanalytic Contributions Toward an Understanding of Personality Development; Vol. 3, Adulthood and Aging.* Ed. Stanley Greenspan and George Pollock. Maryland: U.S. Dept. of Health and Human Services, 1981.

Halifax, Joan. "Elders as Healers." Omega Institute Conference on Conscious Aging (May 1, 1992). Denver: Sounds True Conference Recordings, 1992.

Hamilton, Edith. *Mythology: Timeless Tales of Gods and Heroes.* New York: Mentor Books, 1953.

Hanbrich, W.S. *Medical Meanings: A Glossary of Word Origins.* New York: Harcourt Brace, 1984.

Hannah, Barbara. *Encounters With the Soul: Active Imagination as Developed by C.G. Jung.* Santa Monica: Sigo Press, 1981.

_____. *Jung: His Life and Work: A Biographical Memoir.* New York: G.P. Putnam's Sons, 1976.

Harding, M. Esther. *The Way of All Women.* New York: Putnam, 1970.

_____. *Woman's Mysteries: Ancient and Modern.* New York: Harper, 1971.

_____. *The Value and Meaning of Depression.* New York: The Analytical Psychology Club of New York, Inc., 1970.

Herzog, E. *Psyche and Death.* Dallas: Spring Publications, 1983.

Hollis, James. *The Middle Passage: From Misery to Meaning in Midlife.* Toronto: Inner City Books, 1993.

Huyck, Margaret, and Hoyer, William. *Adult Development and Aging.* Belmont, CA: Wadsworth Publishing Co., 1982.

Jaffé, Aniela, ed. *C.G. Jung: Word and Image* (Bollingen Series XCVII:2). Princeton: Princeton University Press, 1979.

Jung, C.G. *The Collected Works* (Bollingen Series XX), 20 vols. Trans. R.F.C. Hull. Ed. H. Read, M. Fordham, G. Adler, Wm. McGuire. Princeton: Princeton University Press, 1953-1979.

_____. *The Freud/Jung Letters* (Bollingen Series XCIV). Ed. William McGuire. Princeton: Princeton University Press, 1974.

_____. *Kundalini: Notes on the Seminar Given with Prof. J.W. Hauer.*

Zürich, 1932. Mimeographed.

_____. *Letters* (Bollingen Series XCV). 2 vols. Princeton: Princeton University Press, 1973.

_____. *Man and His Symbols.* New York: Doubleday and Co., 1964.

_____. *Memories, Dreams, Reflections.* Ed. Aniela Jaffé. New York: Random House, 1963.

_____. *Modern Man in Search of a Soul.* New York: Harcourt, Brace & Co., 1933.

_____. *Seminar on Dream Analysis* (Bollingen Series XCIX). Princeton: Princeton University Press, 1984.

_____. *The Visions Seminars: Notes of the Seminars, 1930-1934.* 2 vols. Zürich: Spring Publications, 1976.

Jung, Emma. *Animus and Anima: Two Essays.* Zürich: Spring Publications, 1978.

Jung, Emma, and von Franz, Marie-Louise. *The Grail Legend.* Trans. Andrea Dykes. Boston: Sigo Press, 1986.

Kerényi, Carl. *Eleusis: Archetypal Image of Mother and Daughter.* Trans. Ralph Manheim. New York: Schocken, 1977.

Kerényi, Carl, and Jung, C.G. *Two Essays on a Science of Mythology: The Myths of the Divine Child and the Divine Maiden.* New York: Harper, 1963.

Klein, Melanie. *Narrative of a Child Analysis.* New York: Dell Publishing, 1975.

Klossowski de Rola, Stanislas. *The Golden Game: Alchemical Engravings of the Seventeenth Century.* New York: George Braziller, Inc., 1988.

Knight, Richard Payne. *The Symbolical Language of Ancient Art and Mythology.* New York: J.W. Bouton, 1892.

Kreinheder, Albert. *Body and Soul: The Other Side of Illness.* Toronto: Inner City Books, 1991.

Krishna, Gopi. *Kundalini: The Revolutionary Energy in Man.* Psychological commentary by James Hillman. London: Shambhala, 1971.

Kurtz, Ron, and Prestera, Hector. *The Body Reveals: What Your Body Says About You.* New York: Harper and Row, 1984.

Lao Tze. *Tao de Ching: The Book of the Way and Its Virtue.* Trans. J. Duyvendak. London: John Murray, Ltd., 1954.

Larousse Egyptian Mythology. New York: Tudor Publishing, 1965.

Lieberman, M. "Psychological Correlates of Impending Death: Some Preliminary Observations." In *Middle Age and Aging*. Ed. Bernice Neugarten. Chicago: University of Chicago Press, 1973.

Longfellow, Henry Wadsworth. *Longfellow's Poems*. Boston: Tichnor and Fields, 1856.

MacDuff, Alistair. *Lords of the Stone: An Anthology of Eskimo Sculpture*. N. Vancouver: Whitecap Books, 1983.

Maddox, G. "Activity and Morale: A Longitudinal Study of Selected Elderly Subjects." In *Social Forces*, vol. 42, no. 2 (1963).

Mankowitz, Ann. *Change of Life: Dreams and the Menopause*. Toronto: Inner City Books, 1984.

Mayor, A. Hyatt, ed. *Hokusai* (with woodcuts from *Brave Warriors of Japan*, 1836). Metropolitan Museum of Art Calendar, 1967.

McNeely, Deldon Anne. *Touching: Body Therapy and Depth Psychology*. Toronto: Inner City Books, 1987.

Mindell, Arnold. *Dreambody: The Body's Role in Revealing the Self.* Boston: Sigo Press, 1982.

Neugarten, Bernice. "Time, Age and the Life Cycle." In *The American Journal of Psychiatry*, vol. 136, no. 7 (1979).

_____. ed. *Middle Age and Aging*. Chicago: University of Chicago Press, 1973.

Neumann, Erich. *Art and the Creative Unconscious*. New York: Harper and Row, 1959.

_____. *The Great Mother: An Analysis of the Archetype* (Bollingen Series XLVII). Princeton: Princeton University Press, 1955.

_____. "The Moon and Matriarchal Consciousness." In *Dynamic Aspects of the Psyche: Selections from Past* Springs. New York: Analytical Psychology Club, 1956.

_____. *The Origins and History of Consciousness* (Bollingen Series XLII). Trans. R.F.C. Hull. Princeton: Princeton University Press, 1954.

_____. "Psychological Stages of Feminine Development." In an extract from *Psychologie des Weiblichen*. Trans. R. Jacobson. Zürich: Rascher Verlag, 1953.

New Larousse Encyclopedia of Mythology. London: Paul Hamlyn, 1960.

Perera, Sylvia Brinton. *Descent to the Goddess: A Way of Initiation for*

Women. Toronto: Inner City Books, 1981.

Rinpoche, Sogyal. *The Tibetan Book of Livng and Dying.* Ed. Patrick Gaffney and Andrew Harvey. San Francisco: Harper Collins, 1992.

Rubin, Lillian. *Women of a Certain Age: The Midlife Search for Self.* New York: Harper Colophon, 1979.

Samuels, Andrew. *Jung and the Post-Jungians.* London: Routledge and Kegan Paul, 1985.

_____. *The Plural Psyche: Personality, Morality and the Father.* London: Routledge and Kegan Paul, 1989.

_____. ed. *The Father.* New York: New York University Press, 1986.

Schectman, Jacqueline. *The Stepmother in Fairytales.* Boston: Sigo Press, 1993.

Schwartz-Salant, Nathan. *The Borderline Personality: Vision and Healing.* Wilmette, IL: Chiron Publications, 1989.

Scott-Maxwell, Florida. "We Are the Sum of Our Days." In *The Listener,* October 1954. Reprinted in *Harper's Bazaar,* October 1956.

Schaffer, Ulrich. *Surprised By Light.* New York: Harper and Row, 1980.

Sharp, Daryl. *The Survival Papers: Anatomy of a Midlife Crisis.* Toronto: Inner City Books, 1988.

Sontag, Susan. *Illness as Metaphor.* New York: Vintage Books, 1979.

Stein, Murray. *In Midlife: A Jungian Perspective.* Dallas: Spring Publications, 1983.

Stein, Robert. "Body and Psyche: An Archetypal View of Psychosomatic Phenomena." In *Spring 1976.*

Stevens, Anthony. *Archetypes: A Natural History of the Self.* New York: William Morrow, 1982.

Storm, Hyemeyohsts. *Seven Arrows.* New York: Harper and Row, 1972.

Turner, Victor. "Betwixt and Between: The Liminal Period in *Rites de Passage.*" In *The Forest of Symbols.* Ithaca, NY: Cornell University Press, 1967.

Ulanov, Ann, and Ulanov, Barry. *The Witch and the Clown: Two Archetypes of Human Sexuality.* Wilmette, IL: Chiron Publications, 1987.

Van der Post, Laurens. *Jung and the Story of Our Time.* New York: Pantheon, 1975.

von Franz, Marie-Louise. *C.G. Jung: His Myth in Our Time.* Trans. William Kennedy. New York: C.G. Jung Foundation, 1975.

_____. *On Dreams and Death.* Boston: Shambhala Publications, 1984.

_____. *Shadow and Evil in Fairy Tales.* Zürich: Spring Publications, 1974.

Wagner, Suzanne. *Matter of Heart.* Film script. Dir. and ed. Mark Whitney. Los Angeles: C.G. Jung Institute of Los Angeles, 1983.

Walker, Barbara. *The Crone: Woman of Age, Wisdom, and Power.* New York: Harper and Row, 1985.

_____. *The Woman's Encyclopedia of Myths and Secrets.* New York: Harper and Row, 1983.

Weigle, M. *Spiders and Spinsters: Women and Mythology.* Albuquerque: University of New Mexico Press, 1985.

Wheelwright, Jane Hollister. *For Women Growing Older: The Animus.* Houston: C.G. Jung Educational Center, 1984.

_____. "Old Age and Death." Tape of lecture at the Los Angeles Jung Institute, 1981. Published in *Quadrant,* vol. 16, no. 1 (Spring 1983).

Williams, Donald Lee. *Border Crossings: A Psychological Perspective on Carlos Castaneda's Path of Knowledge.* Toronto: Inner City Books, 1981.

Winnicott, D.W. "Ego Distortion in Terms of True and False Self." In *The Maturational Processes and the Facilitating Environment.* New York: International University Press, 1965.

Wolff, Toni. "Structural Forms of the Feminine Psyche." Berne, Switzerland: Herausgeber G.H. Graber, 1956.

_____. *The Collected Papers of Toni Wolff.* Ed. Robert Hinshaw and Marilyn Auer. Einsiedeln, Switzerland: Daimon Verlag, in production.

Woodman, Marion. *Addiction to Perfection: The Still Unravished Bride.* Toronto: Inner City Books, 1982.

_____. *Conscious Femininity: Interviews with Marion Woodman.* Toronto: Inner City Books, 1993.

Young-Eisendrath, Polly, and Wiedemann, Florence. *Female Authority: Empowering Women Through Psychotherapy.* New York: Guilford Press, 1987.

Zeigler, Alfred. *Archetypal Medicine.* Trans. Gary Hartman. Dallas: Spring Publications, 1983.

Index